LESS *IS* MORE

"Won't it take too much time to simp...y my life?"
All it takes is a few minutes a day to sort through a lifetime of clutter.

"Is the 'simple' life boring?"
Not at all. Besides, having less on your mind might make room for creative thoughts.

"Are people who live simply underachievers?"
Simplicity is about scaling down, not dropping out.

"What if that Elvis Christmas record album increases in value?"
For whom? Are you really planning to resell it? Or for that matter ever listen to it again?

"Why simplify?"
It saves time, money, and energy. It makes you more creative, organized, energized, and efficient—and it allows you to focus on the important things in life.

ANY MORE QUESTIONS?

30 DAYS TO A SIMPLER LIFE HAS THE ANSWERS.

CRIS EVATT and **CONNIE COX** are both authors and lecturers on the art of simpler living. While Cris concentrates on the fundamentals of minimalism in achieving simplification, Connie focuses on organizational techniques for balancing more hectic lifestyles. Connie and Cris co-wrote *Simply Organized!*, in which they combined their different techniques for simpler living.

Books by Cris Evatt
How to Organize Your Closet . . . and Your Life!
How to Pack Your Suitcase . . . and Other Travel Tips!
The Givers & the Takers
Opposite Sides of the Bed
Simply Organized!

Books by Connie Cox
Home Management Systems Notebook
Simply Organized!

30 DAYS TO A SIMPLER LIFE

CONNIE COX AND CRIS EVATT

A PLUME BOOK

PLUME
Published by the Penguin Group
Penguin Putnam Inc., 375 Hudson Street,
New York, New York 10014, U.S.A.
Penguin Books Ltd, 27 Wrights Lane,
London W8 5TZ, England
Penguin Books Australia Ltd, Ringwood,
Victoria, Australia
Penguin Books Canada Ltd, 10 Alcorn Avenue,
Toronto, Ontario, Canada M4V 3B2
Penguin Books (N.Z.) Ltd, 182–190 Wairau Road,
Auckland 10, New Zealand

Penguin Books Ltd, Registered Offices:
Harmondsworth, Middlesex, England

First published by Plume, an imprint of Dutton NAL,
a member of Penguin Putnam Inc.

First Printing, October, 1998
10   9   8   7   6   5   4

Ⓟ REGISTERED TRADEMARK—MARCA REGISTRADA

LIBRARY OF CONGRESS CATALOGING-IN-PUBLICATION DATA:

Cox, Connie.
    30 days to a simpler life / Connie Cox and Cris Evatt.
        p.   cm.
    Includes bibliographical references.
    ISBN 0-452-28013-3
    1. Home economics.   2. Time management.   I. Evatt, Cris.   II. Title.
TX147.C862   1998
640'.43—dc21
                                                                        98-18436
                                                                        CIP

Printed in the United States of America
Set in Sabon
Designed by Leonard Telesca

BOOKS ARE AVAILABLE AT QUANTITY DISCOUNTS WHEN USED TO PROMOTE PRODUCTS OR SERVICES. FOR INFORMATION PLEASE WRITE TO PREMIUM MARKETING DIVISION, PENGUIN PUTNAM INC., 375 HUDSON STREET, NEW YORK, NEW YORK 10014.

For Jon, Dave, Theo, and Candice

Certain environments, certain modes of life, and certain rules of conduct are more conducive to inner and outer harmony than others. There are, in fact, certain roads that one may follow. Simplification is one of them.

—Anne Morrow Lindbergh

Contents

Before You Begin 1
Simplify Your Life Day by Day 9

DAY 1   Fill a Shopping Bag 11

DAY 2   Practice Living Without It! 15

DAY 3   Think Before You Buy 21

DAY 4   Create a Serene Bedroom 27

DAY 5   Organize Your Closet 32

DAY 6   Dress with Less 38

DAY 7   Transform Your Bathroom 45

DAY 8   Streamline Your Kitchen 50

DAY 9   Fix Quick and Healthy Meals 55

DAY 10   Revise Your Living Spaces 64

DAY 11   Consider Minimalism 69

DAY 12   Simplify Your Mind 74

DAY 13   Edit Your Projects 81

DAY 14   Combat Information Overload 86

DAY 15   Design Simple Systems 93

DAY 16   Set Up an Efficient Office 101

DAY 17   Organize Your Computer Life 111

DAY 18   Go for Financial Freedom 116

DAY 19   Run Fewer Errands 123

DAY 20   Be Mindful, Savor Time 131

DAY 21   Travel Light in Style 136

DAY 22   Keep Track of Your Valuables 143

DAY 23   Give Vanishing Gifts 147

DAY 24   Create Hassle-Free Holidays 152

DAY 25   Enjoy Your Photos and Mementos 156

DAY 26   Pare Down Your Garage 164

DAY 27   Make Landscaping Easier 169

DAY 28   Get Physical! 175

DAY 29   Find Out What Works 180

DAY 30   Get a Little Help from Your Friends 183

Appendix 191

Books, Newsletters, and Websites 193

Before You Begin

Life is complicated.

But you have already taken the first step toward making it simpler. You bought this book. Congratulations! You are about to embark on a road to a simpler life.

On your journey, you will let go of things that are stressful, distracting, and uncomfortable. You will keep what brings joy, contentment, and a sense of well-being. Simplicity is about achieving a higher level of comfort.

Simplicity is about eliminating the excess, so you will be free to discover who you really are.

When you bought this book, you may have thought, "Okay, they'll tell me how to run my life!" That's not our intention. Instead, we will share our ideas and encourage you to create your own version of simple living. Call it Signature Simplicity or Personal Style Simplicity, if you will. Use our ideas as raw material for artistic creation.

The degree to which you desire to simplify depends on your goals and lifestyle. "Simplicity requires an individual commitment and an individual program," writes David Shi in *The Simple Life*. There is no single formula, no checklist, for simplifying life.

But you may say, "Why should I go to the trouble? Simplifying is time-consuming." Here is a list of reasons that motivated us to edit our lives and write this book:

Living simply saves time—waste less time on irrelevant activities; work smarter, not harder; make fewer commitments to others and to yourself; have more time for doing what you love.

Simplicity saves money—with less to buy, repair, and insure, it's easier to save money and become financially independent.

Simple solutions are creative—delight in doing things unconventionally, in dramatically new ways.

Simplicity leads to organization—with less clutter (fewer unwanted and unloved possessions), it's easier to become and stay organized.

Simplicity is energy efficient—care for the environment by consuming and wasting less; have time to educate yourself about the state of the Earth.

Simple living is serene—live in a quieter environment, one that allows you to cultivate peace of mind.

Living simply allows you to focus on what's important—by spending less time on mundane maintenance, you will be able to focus on your top priorities.

Before creating your own version of simple living, read about The Five Types of Simplifiers—Serene, Comfort-Seeking, Downshifted, Elegant, and Organized Simplifiers. Perhaps one style will resonate with you, or you may find yourself identifying with more than one style.

The Serene Simplifier

The Serene Simplifier's world is peaceful. It is marked by an absence or cessation of motion. Stillness. Her home features little or no ornamentation. Bare walls and plush, oversized furnishings sustain her. Color is used sparingly.

"I have a real problem with loud colors and dizzy, patterned walls," she says. "I want all of my rooms to feel restful, especially after a hectic day at work."

To keep her life serene, she questions everything she brings into her home. She asks, "Do I really need this? Is there something I can use instead? Will it affect my peace of mind?" She controls her material life. It doesn't control her.

This woman (or man) is a big fan of *minimalism*—the school of abstract painting and sculpture that emphasizes extreme simplification of form by using basic shapes and monochromatic palettes. She might be familiar with the works of Bauhaus artists and architects.

The Serene Simplifier prefers serenity to stimulation. She is easily overwhelmed by bright lights and noise. She avoids artificial stimulants like coffee, drugs, alcohol, and tobacco. She would rather meditate and practice yoga than party, and she would rather read than watch television. Three of her favorite books are Janet Luhrs's *The Simple Living Guide*, Thomas Moore's *Care of the Soul*, and Cecile Andrews's *The Circle of Simplicity*.

The Comfort-Seeking Simplifier

Comfort is her passion. When she shops, she focuses on comfort before cost. For instance, she might buy a super-comfortable sofa and then not have enough money for an armchair. So what does she do? She lives with a deck chair until she can afford a model that meets her standards of comfort, knowing that if she tolerates discomfort, she will get it.

She never settles for semi-comfortable.

All of her clothes are comfortable. She never wears anything that pulls, pinches, scratches, or restricts movement. She avoids tight shoes, jackets, and waistbands. Her handbag is soft and smooth, beautiful and efficient.

When she grocery shops, she doesn't look for bargains or bother with coupons. She is an event-shopper. She might buy a little jar of sundried tomatoes, a bunch of fresh basil, and some fresh-made pasta for her evening meal. She likes comfort foods such as risotto, bean soup, and chicken pot pies. Her favorite desserts are apple crisp and bread pudding. On the weekends, she bakes bread because she loves the smell.

She keeps a running list of simple pleasures.

When she chooses a project, she immerses herself in it, completes it, and lets it go. For instance, when she buys a new book, she reads it from cover to cover, then passes it on. Books on her reading list might include Alecia Beldegreen's *The Bed*, Jennifer Louden's *The Comfort Book*, and Susannah Seton's *Simple Pleasures of the Garden*.

She doesn't have a pile of backlogged projects. She is not scattered and rarely acts out of guilt. Her vocabulary is sprinkled with "I love . . . ," "I enjoy . . . ," and "I'm excited about . . ."

The Downshifted Simplifier

After tasting the bittersweet life in the fast lane, the Downshifted Simplifier quit her demanding job, sold her mortgaged house, and used her equity to purchase a smaller home in a small town where there is no smog, no crime, and no commuter traffic.

Formerly a nine-to-fiver, she was inspired to downscale by the bestseller *Your Money or Your Life* by Joe Dominguez and Vicki Robin. "I read it and then cut up six credit cards," she says, "and I no longer watch the shopping channel."

The Downshifter takes good care of the few things she owns. Her tactics for saving money include bartering, buying foods in bulk, and making her own skin care products.

Since she downscaled, she spends less time maintaining her possessions and more time walking, biking, and enjoying time to herself. The rooms of her house are open, airy, and bright. Her lifestyle is informal, and friends are always welcome.

The Downshifter tends to be an active member of an environmental organization. After the Kyoto Conference on Global Warming, she spent several Saturdays planting trees.

Beside her bed sit well-worn copies of Duane Elgin's *Voluntary Simplicity*, David Pearson's *The Natural House Book*, Jacqueline Blix and David Heitmiller's *Getting a Life*, and Amy Dacyczyn's *Tightwad Gazettes*.

The Elegant Simplifier

The Elegant Simplifier is very artistic. Her hobbies include art history, interior design, and flower arranging. Because her taste is impeccable, she can readily discern the difference between good, better, and best.

Each year, she buys a few stylish garments to update her wardrobe. She chooses classic style over trendy. Her clothes are timeless in cut, color, and pattern—she rarely buys throwaway items. Her belts, shoes, handbags, and jewelry are enduring.

She insists on quality. For example, she would buy one high-quality cashmere sweater rather than three mediocre, less expensive ones. She thinks like a wealthy woman even though her income may be modest.

Her home furnishings reflect her preference for quality over quantity. She is more apt to recover an old well-constructed sofa than to run out and buy a new one. She chooses fabrics that are smooth, not heavily textured.

She says, "A cluttered room is the antithesis of elegance."

You won't see hundreds of tiny trinkets in her home. Just a few large objets d'art gleaming in the sun. You also won't see hundreds of family photographs. Instead, you might see one or two extra-large, elegantly framed photographs of vacations or special family celebrations. If you visited her home, the word "restraint" would come to mind. Elegance is understated.

What does she enjoy reading? On her coffee table, you'll find such books as Lillian Too's *Feng Shui*, Julia Cameron's *The Artist's Way*, and Alexandra Stoddard's *Living Beautifully*.

The Organized Simplifier

In sharp contrast to the women above, the Organized Simplifier is involved, in motion, and in the flow of life. She has a demanding job and busy social schedule. She loves her busy life, so don't tell her to slow down.

In the Victorian Era, she probably had seven kids, operated a soup kitchen for the poor, and had musicales in her home on Sunday afternoons. Someone would play the piano, others would sing. Yes, she is highly organized.

She designs clever systems for absolutely everything.

Systems for cooking, laundry, finances, travel, you name it. Her prized systems enable her to have a "balanced life" with ample time for her passions, family, and friends—and time to gather her thoughts.

The Organized Simplifier thrives on stimulation and orchestrates it masterfully. She is a vigilant gatekeeper who screens out unwanted intrusions such as junk mail and uninvited solicitations.

Also, she's an "early adopter." She loves to experiment with new things and ideas. She's a "foodie" who discovered basil pesto, sundried tomatoes, and balsamic vinegar before Safeway. She's a "health nut" who touted ginseng, echinacea, and goldenseal early on. She's a "techie" who had an e-mail address before the rest. Her cutting-edge lifestyle appeals to people who want to gain control of a very full life.

Her favorite books are Beryl Bender Birch's *Power Yoga*, Stephen R. Covey's *Daily Reflections for Highly Effective People*, and Adair Lara's *Slowing Down in a Speeded Up World*.

Which Type of Simplifier Is Cris?

During the eighties, Cris and her husband, Dave, sailed from San Francisco to the South Pacific on their 43 by 11–foot sailboat. Half of the boat's interior space was used for six berths, an engine, and lockers for sails and spare parts. In such small living quarters, there was no room for clutter. Though Cris lived simply on her voyage, she soon learned that the people of Fiji and Tonga could live with far less.

Upon returning home, Cris and her husband moved into a 590-square-foot red-shingled cottage with a front porch, kitchen, bathroom, one bedroom, two closets, small living room, and back deck. "Because my house is so small, I can vacuum it in fifteen minutes!" Cris says.

For the past twenty years, Cris has spent time simplifying every aspect of her home. She has found that solid neutral colors are easier to live with than busy prints. "I like interiors that don't compete with nature's rich tapestry of patterns, texture, and color," she says. "My sparsely filled cupboards store items like white dishes, cream-colored sheets, and light green bath towels."

Early on, Cris was struck by the realization that *a room with one thousand items is more difficult to manage than a room with only ten.* This image continually inspires her to review her possessions. "If I don't use it or love it, I get rid of it. Immediately!"

Which type is Cris? She's the Serene Simplifier, and secondarily, the Downshifted Simplifier.

Which Type Is Connie?

Connie enjoys the fact that her lifestyle is different from Cris's and thinks their differences make the process of writing together exciting. "We laugh at our differences," she says. "She's into sparse, plain, and natural, and I'm into space, pattern, and color."

Connie has always chosen to have a busy and varied life. In her thirties, she attended law school and became an estate planning attorney. Prior to that she was a professional fund-raiser and before that a junior high school teacher. She is married to a trial lawyer, and between them they have four children. She is an active volunteer in her children's schools and community.

Today, Connie is an author and the owner of Home Management Systems, a business which produces workshops, lectures, and consultations on how to simplify, systematize, and delegate at home and in the workplace. Each participant in the workshop receives a comprehensive notebook with forms for managing all aspects of a personal life, such as finances, travel, and household help. Connie has spent the past 15 years helping people edit and systematize their busy lifestyles.

Connie sees life as a game, a sporting match in which the challenge is to see how much she can do in a systematic, organized manner. Connie's own systems are constantly being honed and edited. The trick, she says, is to stay balanced—to balance the need for stimulation with the need to feel centered and whole. "Sometimes I forget who I am because I am out in the world too much, and sometimes I become too inward and lack worldly stimulation."

Connie doesn't want to be stuck in old ways of thinking. "I love to be on the cutting edge. I want to learn about things as they first happen. New ideas. New technology. That's why I attend computer shows, study the Enneagram, and belong to an investment club."

Which type of simplifier is Connie? She identifies most with the Organized Simplifier and then the Elegant Simplifier.

Simplify Your Life Day by Day

Simple living is the perfect antidote for a stressful life.

Simplicity means paring down, getting back to the basics, eliminating all but the essentials. It means having more free time, energy, money, and space for your passions. Time for tap dancing, tai chi, traveling, socializing, or singing in a choir. Or time for pursuing a new career or advancing your present one.

Lao-tzu said, "Accomplish a great task by a series of small acts."

Our book is based on the premise that 30 days and 30 tasks, along with tips, quotes, and inspirational stories, can start you on a simpler path. We have designed each task to be done in about an hour.

In the tip section of each chapter, we suggest that you make a red check mark in the boxes beside the tips you wish to recall. Why red? Red will make the tips easier to find.

At the very end of most chapters is a short section titled "For Serious Simplifiers Only!" This section is designed for people who want to simplify their lives to the nth degree—people who are willing to break their attachments to *everything* that complicates it. The faint-hearted need not comply.

Simplifying is like exercise. You cannot go to a spa for a week and become toned, firm, and fit for life. Likewise, you cannot get your life in shape in a week, a month, or even a year. You must chip away at both, working at each in small bite-sized chunks, within the framework of your life.

After you have completed tasks from this book, make simplifying a part of your routine. Dedicate an hour to it a few times a week. After a while, simplification will become a habit. A self-perpetuating process. Soon you will become skilled at culling out the inconsequential from the basic.

The tasks in our book are cumulative. As you let things go, you will learn about your preferences—your likes and dislikes. As your life becomes simpler, you have fewer things to delete, monitor, and maintain. Clutter will no longer rear its ugly head. When you reach this stage, you will have time to pursue your passions with gusto. You will be able to live your life out loud.

Now it's time to begin.

DAY 1

Fill a Shopping Bag

Task: *Today, gather up a bagful of things you no longer love and use. First, find a shopping bag, trash bag, or cardboard box. Next, fill it with giveaways or throwaways from around your house. Gather unwanted stuff from anywhere in your home or garage. Look under sinks, in closets, into drawers, and under the bed. No space is off limits. Finally, put the stuff into your car's trunk to be recycled. This task could take from five minutes to an hour, depending on how decisive you are. Fill as many bags as you can in one hour.*

By simplifying you will get control of your possessions—layer by layer, drawer by drawer, closet by closet. If you were to fill one shopping bag weekly for a year, you would rid yourself of fifty-two bags of clutter. Amazing, isn't it? After that, you can keep clutter under control by filling a bag monthly.

One of Cris's favorite pastimes is looking for things to toss. "My goal is to be conscious of everything I own," she says. "Living with less enables me to live more spontaneously." When Cris runs out of things to toss, she helps others dejunk their lives.

Schedule thrift store drop-offs and a garage sale on your calendar, if it makes editing your life easier. Make simplification a habit, a hobby, a challenging game. Create space around your things, so you can breathe freely.

Simplifying makes room for energy to flow freely through your life.

Myths About Living Simply

Living things bud, grow, flourish, and die. Everything on Earth has a life cycle. Ask yourself, "Do my possessions and interests flow through my life or clog it?" We have discovered several myths that keep people from simplifying.

Myth 1: "Living simply is an Outward Bound experience"

To live simply, you don't have to live like a nun or hermit, or go without a computer or cappuccino machine. Your home and office should be comfortable and efficient, not challenging. For Connie, simplifying means having useful systems to manage her laundry, finances, phone numbers, theater tickets, and frequent flyer miles. For Cris, it means having few possessions, a small, well-crafted home, and five egg-producing chickens in the backyard. Simplicity means different things to different people. But to everyone, it means less stress.

Simplicity is about achieving a higher level of comfort, whatever that means for you.

Myth 2: "It'll take too much time to simplify my life"

Yes, it takes time to simplify. That's why we wrote a book with one-hour tasks. Spend only an hour at a time sorting through clutter. Don't become overwhelmed.

If you simplify your life, you will save time. You will stop wasting time looking for things. You will possess less and each item you own will have its own special place, not a random destination. Have you ever frantically searched for your keys, a birth certificate, or a pink slip for a car? Not only do these episodes take time, but they can throw your stomach into nasty little knots.

Ultimately, simplifying saves time.

Myth 3: "Simple living is boring"

Boredom is bad? We don't think so. Boredom can lead to creativity. Gertrude Stein said, "It takes a lot of time to be a genius, you have to sit around so much doing nothing, really doing nothing." Think of all the good ideas you get while you are taking a walk or standing in the shower. Boredom gives you time to appreciate the beauty of the world, to notice the smallest things. Learn to welcome moments when nothing is on your mind.

Simple living makes space for new ideas and opportunities.

Myth 4: "I will be deprived of things I love"

If deprivation has been or is an issue for you, then simplification may sound like another way to feel poor. It's not. It's about feeling richer by choosing quality over quantity. It's about having more wonderful things in your life and fewer things that don't bring joy.

We have learned that one terrific outfit with complementary shoes, belt, handbag, and a couple of harmonious tops is more enriching than a closet full of passable, mismatched separates. Or one beautiful pen can be more pleasurable to own than a million ballpoints.

It takes the same amount of money to own one great thing as several mediocre ones.

Myth 5: "People who live simply are dropouts and slackers"

Let go of the notion that gentle, relaxed people can't be super-achievers. You don't have to travel in the fast lane to get things done. A simpler lifestyle is energizing—not enervating! It's about balancing work and play. It's not about escapism. Simplicity means deliberately owning less and working less, so you can devote more time to your creativity and spirituality, your friends and family, or a social cause.

Simplicity is about scaling down, not dropping out.

Myth 6: "Simplicity means I can't have new things"

Simplicity means having more time for exciting new things—new hobbies, new friends, new computer programs, and new travel destinations. Of course, too many new things and activities can create anxiety and more work. To integrate the new into your life, shuck off the old. Set new priorities. Choose a few things. Keep evolving, adding and subtracting. Create a dynamic lifestyle, not a boring or crazy one.

Simplicity is revitalizing.

For Serious Simplifiers Only!

If you are really serious about simplifying your life, take a giant step today and fill ten—not one—shopping bags with unused, unloved things from around your house. Immediately afterward, drop those bags off at a thrift shop.

∽

The cost of a thing is the amount of what I call life
which is required to be exchanged for it,
immediately or in the long run.

—Henry David Thoreau

DAY 2

Practice Living Without It!

Task: *Today, dejunk one drawer. If you are like most people, messy drawers abound in your kitchen, bedroom, and bathroom. Do the three steps of sorting, recycling, and dealing with ambivalence that are outlined below in "The Mechanics of Simplifying." These simple steps will help you simplify and organize every area of your life.*

Is the state of a person's mind reflected by the condition of his drawers? Does a person with crammed, disorganized drawers have an unruly, jabbering mind? And does a person with orderly, sparsely filled drawers have a calm mind? Perhaps. If you simplify your drawers, your mind might begin to clear, too.

Streamlining a junk drawer can be your mission today. With its jumbled assemblage of screws, coupons, ballpoints, rubber bands, warranties, bits of string, dead batteries, and mysterious keys, it symbolizes chaos. If you are missing something, it may be in your junk drawer—but don't count on it!

A junk drawer is a fitting metaphor for a complicated life.

The Mechanics of Simplifying

In the early eighties, Cris discovered four easy steps for simplifying life. The people in Connie's seminars have reported, over the years, that these steps made a huge difference in their lives. Because of their enthusiasm, we featured them in our first book, *Simply Organized!*, and are including them again in this chapter. Use these steps to conquer your files, closets, drawers, garage, and any other area you wish to simplify.

Step 1. Sort your things into three piles

Choose an area (today it's your drawer) to simplify. Pick up each item in it and ask yourself: "Do I love and use it?" "Do I want to recycle it?" "Do I feel ambivalent about it?" Don't rush this step.

- **The Love and Use Pile:** (Certainty) Fill this pile with your terrific things. The things you use and enjoy. The crème de la crème.
- **The Recycle Pile:** (Certainty) You are eager to toss out this stuff. Why haven't you done it before today? Who cares? Now is the perfect time.
- **The Ambivalence Pile:** (Uncertainty) Ambivalent items are things you both like and dislike. They can drive you crazy because you don't know whether to keep them or to let them go. Creating this pile is the key to uncomplicating your life. But first, read about why you have so many things in this category.

If I get rid of it, I'm throwing money away. No, you will save money. If you get rid of it, you won't have to clean it, store it, insure it, repair it, refill it, or look at it. But if money is an issue, sell it or donate it for a tax deduction. Pass on your rejects while they are still useful to others. No one wants your black-and-white television, old record player, or wooden tennis racquet now. And large objects such as used sofas, old refrigerators, and rusty lawn furniture can cost more to store than replace, if in fact you ever do.

I may use it in the future. Yes, it's true you may use it in the future, and then again, you may not find it in the future. And if you do find it, it may be completely out of style, like a recipe using lots of fat or an umbrella with huge ducks printed on it.

It reminds me of the past. Memories, memories. Of course, they're important. We love to look at things from our past and from our parents' past as well. Photos, awards, postcards, and newspaper clippings are great to keep when they are organized, accessible, and displayed so they may be enjoyed. But an old sweater or a stuffed mongoose? Take them to a thrift shop. Learn to balance the weight of the past against the lightness of the future.

But it was a gift. Yes, it was a gift and, no doubt, a thoughtful one. But did it bring joy or add stress to your life? There are three things you can do with a burdensome gift: (1) Exchange it for something you want. (2) Give it to someone who will use it. (3) Donate it to a charity. It's okay to get rid of gifts. Gifts are symbols of love. Keep the love and let go of the symbols.

I must find someone to give it to. Do you really want to think about giving the right item to the right person at the right time? "Will she use it?" "Is it his size?" "Does she have one?" "Will he take it as an insult?" Sounds like another job. Delegate that job to thrift shops. A preoccupation with finding the right home for something may be a subtle way of extending control over it. Instead, gain control of the possessions you use and love.

I'm going to gain/lose weight. Eliminate clothes that don't fit. Toss them today or store them away. Look great at your current weight, and then when you lose, streamline your wardrobe again. Our friend Josie held on to her high school jeans, vowing, pledging, and swearing she would wear them again. They tortured her for years until she finally surrendered, joined a weight-loss group, and focused on a healthier relationship with food. She tossed the jeans with a sigh of relief, and, in a few months, dropped the extra pounds.

I own, therefore I am. "Our true identity is much larger than any that can be fashioned through the most opulent levels of material consumption," says Duane Elgin, the author of *Voluntary Simplicity*.

But it's a souvenir! Some people go to Niagara Falls, where they spend more time looking at souvenirs than the Falls. The next time you return from a trip to a romantic destination, keep the experience in your heart—not on your shelf!

Peer pressure made me buy it. Fill your life with things that you love, *not* what others have. What a shame to maintain, worry about, store, and resent things you don't truly want. Simplicity is about removing the obstacles to self-determination. One of those obstacles is peer pressure.

Buying it was a horrible mistake. What if it's brand-new and you can't take it back? Perhaps you bought a pasta machine that you used once in ten years. Isn't it better to let go of it and learn from it, than live with it forever? We all make mistakes. Don't keep things around that remind you of the error of your ways. Surround yourself with useful and beautiful things that were excellent choices.

I'm going to fix it someday. Put a things-to-be-repaired box in your car. If possible, take these items to a repair shop this week. If you need to call a professional to come to your home, call today. If you think you will never get around to repairing something, move it out and get on with your life. If it's something you rarely use, but can rent or borrow, toss it.

I'm addicted to my stuff. Sandra Felton, the founder of *Messies Anonymous*, a support group based on the AA Twelve Steps, says, "Possessions actually do fill some deep need, soothe some chronic ache, and slake some unseen thirst. However, as with alcohol and other addictive substances, the relief is short lived. As in the case of the alcoholic who sobers up to find his problems worsened by his latest binge, the Messie finds her problem worsened because she has gathered more stuff to live with." Do your possessions make you healthy or make you crazy?

But I have room for it. Don't feel obligated to fill up empty spaces. Empty spaces are the modern equivalent of luxury and with them come opportunities for growth. Our friend Cheryl lines her empty drawers with gorgeous paper and gives herself a thrill by peeking into them when her life feels overwhelming. We kid you not.

Step 2. Create an Ambivalence Center

It is extremely important to separate the things you feel ambivalent about from the things you Love and Use. There is nothing worse than rummaging through things you don't like to find what you need. Store your ambivalent items out of sight—in a storage locker, in a spare room, in the back of the closet, or in a corner of your garage.

Practice living without your ambivalent items.

To create an Ambivalence Center, buy cardboard storage boxes, which cost about $3.00 a piece, label them clearly, and make stacks of four or more. Inside each, place your ambivalent items from all over your house. Collect items that are not being used that you're unwilling to toss. These boxes give your things a transition zone. You can practice living without them. You will not feel deprived of these items because you will still own them.

You will feel lighter.

Author Isak Dinesen said, "I had consented to give away my possessions one by one, as a kind of ransom for my own life, but by the time that I had nothing left, I myself was the lightest thing of all."

Step 3. Remove the Recycle Pile

Put your Recycle Pile into the trunk of your car. Take these items to a thrift store as soon as possible. Lighten your life.

Step 4. Design simple systems

You have one pile left: *The Love and Use Pile.* Put these things away neatly. Or better yet, design a simple system for these items. We will talk in depth about why setting up systems is so important on "Day 15—Design Simple Systems."

For Serious Simplifiers Only!

Tackle at least five drawers today. Be bold. Toss as many items as you possibly can. Make the items remaining in your drawers more accessible by using organizers—small boxes, plastic trays, rectangular baskets—to divide up drawer space. Be ruthless!

If you look at your entire house as one unit of junk, you'll never do anything because the job is too overwhelming. Take it one drawer at a time.

—Janet Luhrs, author of *The Simple Living Guide*

DAY 3

Think Before You Buy

Task: *Create a checklist of questions that will help you decide what to buy and what to forgo. Below, we have listed examples of questions for your list. At the very top of the list, write down your major life goals in sound bites. For example, you might write "get fit," "travel more," or "study wildflowers." Put your list in your wallet so you can consult it when you go shopping. When it comes time to purchase something, determine whether your goals and the purchase are harmonious.*

Each item you buy makes a statement about who you are and what interests you. Buy more things that propel you toward your goals and fewer things that create obstacles.

Think of the time you spend shopping, ordering, storing, cleaning, fixing, sorting, rearranging, insuring, worrying, protecting, upgrading, operating, and learning about your things. Plus, many of these activities may be broken down into additional jobs.

For instance, "cleaning" also involves spotting, soaking, scouring, washing, rinsing, sweeping, vacuuming, dusting, and polishing. If you do all these things, when will you have time for your passions?

Material possessions are a means, not an end. Know which ones you own and which ones own you. To keep from over-accumulating, stall before dashing to the mall. Ask yourself these grounding questions:

Will it enhance my goals? When you are tempted to purchase something, determine whether the item will distract you or propel you toward your noblest ambitions.

Will it create more work? Who will maintain it? If it will be you, are you willing to spend the time to do it?

Do I need it? If it's clothing, will it fill a missing part of your wardrobe or be an unnecessary duplicate? If it's for your home, is it "cute" or an essential addition? If it replaces something you have, are you willing to scrap the original?

Is it truly a bargain? If it were full price, would you buy it? Would you save for it? If you wouldn't, then it's not such a good deal. Bargains are deceiving.

Do I think it will make my life easier? Many purchases create work. Make a distinction between what serves you and what enslaves you. Connie has self-watering planters, which require water only once a month. This clever invention makes her life easier. Kate doesn't own plants. This makes her life easier still.

Do I want it because it's trendy? "Trendy" means temporarily in style. Faddish. Exciting today, boring tomorrow. When it goes out of style, will you have the fortitude to recycle it? Or will you keep it and worry about the money you have blown? Learn to discriminate between your fleeting wants and actual needs.

Will it bring my family together or tear us apart? Possessions can cause dissension. Servicing them can interfere with family time together. Our friends John and Karen own a speedboat and spend many happy hours waterskiing, whereas another friend, Wally, says, "Thank you, God," every time he passes someone else's boat. As a former boat owner, he thinks "a boat is a hole in the water into which you pour money." One person's pleasure is another person's pain.

Do I want it because it will make me feel better? Instead of buying something that endures, cheer yourself up with consumables like cut flowers, a massage, or an evening at a comedy club. (Give consumables as gifts, too.) Some people view consumables as a waste of money because they are not lasting—the enjoyment of them is brief. That's the beauty.

Will I have trouble getting rid of it in the future? Many people have storage lockers crammed full of things they cannot toss, but never use. Stored possessions can become a future burden.

By the time we emerge from childhood, we firmly believe that things will bring us happiness. If one thing is fun and gives us pleasure, then more things will certainly increase our pleasure. As we mature, we find this to be untrue. *Having enough is what brings satisfaction.*

How Much Is Enough?

Decisions about bringing material objects into your life cannot be taken lightly. Most items complicate life. To keep life simple, follow this rule—"If it's small, wait a week before buying it. If it's large, wait a month." After time passes, one of these three things often happens:

You lose interest in the product. You think you need a three-hundred-dollar bread maker and, a week later, you are on a diet that excludes bread.

You find something at home that works as well. You find a skirt in the back of your closet that looks great with your new sweater.

You discover something else you would rather have. You stumble upon a better, cheaper pair of hiking boots.

What most of us don't have enough of is time. Stuff takes time. If you want more time, own less stuff.

Ivan's Journey Home

We come into and go out of this world with nothing, so why do we cling to so many things while we are here? When we die our possessions are left at the mercy of relatives who sell them, disperse them, argue about them, toss them in garbage cans, and call the Goodwill truck. The worst part is that we cannot be there to supervise.

Two years ago, Cris drove to Fresno, California, to visit her 78-year-old father, Ivan Peterson, who had been put in a nursing home after a major heart attack. During the visit, he asked her to deal with his belongings. She agreed, knowing that most of them would have to be discarded.

In Ivan's bedroom, hundreds of papers were crammed into four boxes, two filing cabinets, and an old black trunk. He had kept handwritten copies of every letter he had written since the early forties. In his living room, there were twelve boxes of family memorabilia and four stuffed birds. In his kitchen, three boxes of dishes, glasses, and utensils were unopened.

Ivan's things filled a large Dumpster located in the parking lot of his apartment building. The boxes of family mementos filled Cris's car and were taken to her cousin's house to be passed on to his children. She kept one box for herself.

On the following day, she returned to her father's apartment. The landlady told her, "Last night, some of Ivan's papers blew out of the debris box and were scattered all over the parking lot. I got some kids to clean them up." So this is what happens to stuff that is carefully monitored for a lifetime. How sad. Cris's dad passed away three weeks later.

There comes a time when we must continue our journey without our family, friends, and possessions.

If we can't take our stuff with us and life is short, what compels us to covet so many things—and to devote so much time to their upkeep? Perhaps, owning is a habit. Or a cultural value? Or maybe it's genetic? We can't know for sure. But we do know that devoting time to the upkeep of our possessions can distract us from nobler pursuits.

Bertrand Russell said, "It is the preoccupation with possessions, more than anything else, that prevents man [woman] from living freely and nobly." Make freedom from ownership your new status symbol.

Listen to Your Inner Doubts

Can we really know when something—a possession, an activity, a person—will complicate our life? We can because our mind fills with doubts when a complicator arises. Tune in to your inner voice and listen to it when it says:

> When in doubt, don't buy it.
> When in doubt, don't rescue it.
> When in doubt, don't eat it.
> When in doubt, don't marry him.
> When in doubt, don't join it.
> When in doubt, don't subscribe to it.
> When in doubt, don't volunteer for it.
> When in doubt, don't have a child or get a pet.
> When in doubt, don't watch it or listen to it.
> When in doubt, throw it out.

If you listen to your inner doubts throughout your lifetime, you will save a tremendous amount of time, energy, and money.

Shopping Simplifiers

Shopping is really about replenishing what we need and adding what will bring us more peace and joy. Conscientious shopping leads to purchases that give us time—don't steal it!

Make a red check mark by tips that will simplify shopping.

❏ **Carry a list of needs and wants.**
We all buy things we don't really need. To buy only what we need, keep a running To Buy list. Categories can include such things as clothing, house, garden, gifts, and pharmacy items. A grocery list is a must. When you go shopping, use your lists to remember things you absolutely need—like a black belt for your jeans, a gift for a best friend's birthday, or blue towels for the bathroom. Lists can keep you from impulsively buying things not listed. Carry them with you.

❏ **For Serious Simplifiers only!**
Take a month-long sabbatical from buying anything but "perishables"—items you use up quickly like gas, food, flowers, and toiletries. During the month, jot down the nonperishable things you think you need or want. At the end of the month, look at your list and cross off as many items as possible. In our society, most of our needs are wants.

I'd rather have roses on my table than diamonds on my neck.

—Emma Goldman

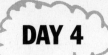

DAY 4

Create a Serene Bedroom

Task: *Today is a great day to edit your sheets and pillowcases. First, take all of your sheets out of your linen closet and put them in three piles: the Recycle Pile, the Ambivalent Pile, and the Love and Use Pile. Second, put the Recyclables in your car's trunk. Third, put the Ambivalent Pile into a lidded box or bag in another closet so you can practice living without these linens. Finally, return the sheets and pillowcases you use to the linen closet.*

Extra linens complicate your life. You only need two sets of sheets and pillowcases for each bed. Store your sets in stacks in your linen closet. Organize and label the stacks by bedroom or size of bed.

Now you are ready to think about your bedroom. Your bedroom is for relaxing, sleeping, and dressing. A comfortable bed and an efficient closet are all you really need to furnish it. Everything else is optional.

Create a fabulous bed with high thread-count cotton sheets that are untreated, undyed, and organic. Return to simpler times when unbleached linens were the norm and creamy tones came from cotton, not chemicals. Atop your luxurious sheets, put a fluffy down comforter, stuffed into a pretty cotton cover, and four standard-sized pillows. Don't go pillow crazy! It takes time, twice a day, to shuffle a dozen pillows in varying shapes and sizes.

A perfect companion for your simple bed is a wall-installed reading lamp. Find one with swivel joints for easy positioning.

For window treatments, try simple roller shades or pleated fabric shades. Drapes hung from wooden rods or wrought iron are simple as well. Make sure your window coverings are easy to operate—you open and close them every morning and evening. Avoid mini-blinds, which collect dust and are hard to clean.

In a pared-down bedroom, bureaus are optional. Built-in closets can store clothing, purses, shoes, and lingerie. Handsome blanket chests can provide hidden storage.

To learn about simple living, study the way the Japanese live. "In a traditional Japanese bedroom, tatami covers the floor, and futons and quilts are stored in cupboards during the day, to be brought out at night," writes Suzanne Slesin in *Japanese Style*.

Cris's bedroom is very Japanese. It is sparsely furnished. The walls are creamy white with matching wainscoting. A beige, speckled carpet partially covers varnished pine floors. She has no dressers, nightstands, or wall hangings. There is simply an attractive (lidded) Tongan laundry basket at the foot of her sturdy oak bentwood bed.

Nothing is harbored under her bed.

Connie's bedroom went through a transformation during the writing of this book. Previously, her bedroom's decor was based on a lively rose and green flowered duvet cover. Now her colors are a soft cream, gold, and green.

To simplify her bedroom even more, Connie removed some of her mementos and changed photo frames to more subdued styles. Then she deleted half of her books and magazines. She kept two nightstands, a writing desk, and two chairs (so family members can congregate in the bedroom). Her bedroom is now more serene and relaxing.

Bedroom Simplifiers

Simplicity means being conscious about every aspect of your life, including the decor of your bedroom.

Make a red check mark by tips that will simplify your bedroom.

❏ **Delete the top sheet—it's optional!**
Scandinavians seldom use top sheets. They sleep under their duvet, or comforter cover, which is washed weekly along with the bottom sheet. Many Americans are beginning to follow their example. Our friend Toni says, "I have a wardrobe of different duvet covers. They serve as a top sheet, bedspread, and color theme for the entire bedroom. In the summer, I remove the comforter and just use the cover." *Embrace new ideas that will simplify your life.*

❏ **Clear the under-the-bed space.**
According to Feng Shui practitioners, storage under the bed stops "chi" (energy) from flowing freely throughout your bedroom. There is only one good reason to put things under the bed: *More space is needed.* If this is the case, purchase a couple of under-the-bed boxes for items that are used occasionally, like ski clothes or extra blankets.

❏ **Build a bedside shelf.**
If you need a surface next to your bed to put things on, like cookies and milk, and do not want a nightstand, build a simple wall-mounted shelf. Paint it the color of your room and it will hardly be noticed. Vacuuming under it will be easy.

❏ **Create a healthy bedroom.**
An array of health problems—like headaches, depression, and itchy eyes—can arise from exposure to seemingly innocent bedroom objects.

- *Avoid brand-new particle-board bedroom sets.* Particle board is made of pressed wood shavings held together with

urea-formaldehyde resins. Furniture made from it emits
toxic gases for several years. If you plan to buy new furniture, choose pieces made of hardwood or wrought iron. Or
buy antique dressers, nightstands, and headboards.

- *Choose natural pillows.* Choose feather, buckwheat, or organic cotton pillows rather than chemically drenched poly-
  ester foam pillows.
- *Look for all-cotton mattress pads.* Cotton mattress pads
  are softer and warmer than synthetic pads. Try the cotton
  chenille mattress pad from the Cuddledown of Maine catalogue (1-800-323-6793).

❏ **Remove any items that don't support dressing, sleeping, or sex.**
Scan your bedroom for objects that do not support the primary
purposes of your bedroom. Your bedroom is not for storing
junk. Attics, offices, libraries, garages, basements, and rented
storage lockers were invented for that purpose. A great book by
a fellow organizer is *More Time for Sex: The Organizing Guide
for Busy Couples* by Harriet Schecter and Vicki Gibbs.

❏ **Don't make your bedroom into a library.**
Dozens of books and magazines stacked around a bedroom remind you of what you think you should be reading, as do bookshelves full of paperbacks. Just keep a few books and current
magazines in your bedroom.

❏ **Keep your office out of your bedroom.**
Bedrooms are for sleeping and relaxing. Offices are for working. Keep the two worlds apart. If possible, do not set up a computer, fax machine, answering machine, or pile of bills in the
bedroom. All of these things are reminders of work to be done.
If you must have your work area in your bedroom because of
space considerations, keep it covered while you sleep.

❏ **Simplify your guest bedroom.**
Connie loves her guest bedroom, which is always ready for unexpected visitors. Her guest bathroom is stocked with small
soaps, hand cream, shampoo, a hair dryer, tissues, and extra

toilet paper. She hangs her guest towels so she can tell if they are fresh. Because her home is organized, she can comfortably share it with others. Cris, on the other hand, shares time at home with loved ones and then escorts them to a bed-and-breakfast.

❑ **Silence a noisy bedroom.**
To make your bedroom quieter, add more absorbent surfaces like thick drapes, fabric wall hangings, soft furnishings, deep-piled area rugs, and a large plant. If your bedroom is far from the entrance and the noisy outside world, you will sleep more soundly.

❑ **Nix the late-night news.**
Connie's friend Lois says, "Don't drift off to sleep after watching a sensational news story about a repulsive crime. Instead, read something entertaining, uplifting, and inspirational."

❑ **For Serious Simplifiers only!**
Create a tranquil bedroom. First, remove the television. Next, remove excess furniture and everything under your bed. Redesign your closet so it can hold clothing that was stored in your dresser. Put a large plant where your dresser used to be. Finally, empty the walls of everything except one serene print, painting, or wall sculpture. Without busy art and bulky furniture, your bedroom will have a spacious, airy feeling.

∾

Beauty of style and harmony and grace and good rhythm depend on simplicity.

—Plato

DAY 5

Organize Your Closet

Task: *Do you ever find yourself saying, "If I'm so smart, why do I have so many clothes and nothing to wear?" After today's task, you will have fewer clothes and more to wear. And it will be easier to use your closet!*

First, sort your clothing into three piles: the Recycle Pile, the Ambivalent Pile, and the Love and Wear Pile. Use the steps in Day 3 as a guide.

Second, put the Recycle Pile into your car to be taken to a thrift shop or a consignment shop. When you give up a garment that no longer feels good to wear, you let go of something that no longer enhances your life.

Third, place the clothes from the Ambivalent Pile onto wire hangers. Hang them in the back of your closet or in another closet. Practice living without these clothes.

Fourth, buy enough wonderful hangers to hold the garments in the Love and Wear Pile. Buy them today, if possible. Finally, hang up your clothes. Tomorrow morning, notice how much easier it is to get dressed. You may find yourself combining colors in new ways.

Organizing your closet may take longer than an hour. You may want to save this task for a Saturday morning.

Soon after Connie started her business, Home Management Systems, she visited her mom, Carolyn, who was feeling frustrated by the contents of her clothes closet. Connie recounts this story:

"Mom and I spent an afternoon scrutinizing her clothes—item by item—as we looked at Cris's book, *How to Organize Your Closet . . . and Your Life!* We laughed over bad purchases and agonized over which clothes should be taken up, let out, re-shaped, or forgotten.

"To decide to take anything but the real losers to a thrift shop was too big a step at that time, so I suggested we stash her Ambivalent items into two large trash bags, and then store the bags in another closet. I urged her to practice living without these clothes—that pleated skirt she once loved, that tired-looking white blouse she could still wear under a sweater, and that flowered dress that was too short but a shame to toss. I urged her to live with the clothes that made her feel fabulous and to store the rest.

"Before I left Mom's house, the two trash bags were placed out of sight and her favorite clothes were hanging neatly by type and color. I reminded her, 'Anytime you want to wear any of the ambivalent clothes, you know where to find them.'

"Two months later, Mom called. 'I took the bags to a thrift shop. I never looked into them once—I didn't miss anything. I love having a closet with just the clothes I love to wear. I could not have gotten rid of those clothes if we had kept them in my closet. I needed to practice living without them.' "

Closet Simplifiers

Closet organizing gadgets are plentiful. Experiment with bins, boxes, baskets, hooks, racks, and shelves from catalogues, hardware stores, bath shops, and specialty closet shops.

Make a red check mark by tips that will simplify your closet.

❑ **Expand your closet's holding capacity—instantly!**
The ideal closet doesn't waste space and its rods don't sag. To expand your closet's holding capacity, effortlessly and inexpensively, hang a spacedoubling rod. Then, to create even more storage space, add a second shelf above the main shelf.

❏ Don't scrimp on hangers.
Simplicity means having one style of hanger. Not a hodgepodge!

- *Buy high-quality hangers.* Hangers last a lifetime. We like plastic hangers with metal hooks and swivel tops, which enable you to turn clothes easily so they face the same direction. A foam piece may be added so clothing won't slide off. These hangers may be ordered in bulk from a wholesale company. We also like plastic tubulars. Buy the sturdiest, thickest tubulars you can find. White and cream hangers do not clash with clothing.
- *Create a special location for empty hangers at one end of your closet.* Then place them there after you remove clothing. Simplicity is about paying attention to the details—and having fewer details to manage.

❏ Arrange your clothing inventively.
Group your clothing in a way that makes sense to you, and then stay with it.

- *Arrange clothes by color*—warms with warms, cools with cools, and neutrals with neutrals.
- *Arrange clothes by type*—pants with pants, shirts with shirts, dresses with dresses, and so on. Within each section, arrange clothing by color.
- *Arrange by function*—work clothes, evening clothes, sports clothes, sleep T-shirts, cold-weather coats. Within each category, arrange by type and color.

❏ Get your shoes off the floor.
Reach up, not down, to get a pair of shoes. If you have a standard closet, place your shoes on the shelf above the rod, and then build another shelf above them. You can store shoes in their boxes, which keeps them from getting dusty. Label the boxes with a description of the shoes. Or, buy a hanging shoe bag. To simplify your shoe wardrobe, wear neutral colored shoes. Exclusively!

❏ **Confront your socks life.**
Ponder each pair, then edit, edit, edit. Eliminate socks that are too loose around your ankles or too tight around your calves or have holes in them. Toss pantyhose that are too tight, too short, or too bizarre a color. Finally, separate your socks by color and type (trouser socks, knee-highs, pantyhose, sports socks). Creating categories simplifies life. To organize your pantyhose after washing, place them in Ziploc bags, separated by color, so that it's easy to find the right pair in the morning. Don't open a new pair of pantyhose until your old ones are worn out. *Acts of restraint simplify life.*

❏ **Get hooked on hooks.**
It is easier to pop something onto a hook than pull out a hanger. Hooks increase your closet's capacity to store things, like hats, belts, scarves, purses, jewelry, and drawstring bags. Hooks can be screwed into the back of the closet doors and around the sides and back of the closet.

❏ **Install towel bars on the back of your closet door.**
Two towel bars fit nicely on the back of a closet door. Towel bars are great for hanging flat things, like tights, pants, and scarves. You can also use them for hanging clothes when you are packing for a trip or planning an outfit for the next day.

❏ **Do less folding.**
To save time, fold your clothes as few times as possible or lay them flat in a drawer. Some items, like underwear, bathing suits, and exercise outfits may be tossed into drawers and not folded at all. And, if each family member were to have one kind of sock, you could toss their socks in their drawer—without creating pairs!

❏ **Hang a drawstring bag for dry cleaning.**
Grab the bag and go to the cleaners without having to search for clothing. To simplify, visit the dry cleaners the same day each week. Return the wire hangers and ask the clerk to omit the long plastic bags. Debra Newsholme, image consultant, says, "Don't dry-clean your clothes until you absolutely have

to. Instead, air them out and steam them. This will reduce the wear on your clothes and the amount of chemicals next to your skin. Plus, you will save on the expense of dry cleaning."

❏ **Use a tablespoon of laundry soap.**
Laundry soap was invented to remove grease and stains. It's not necessary for clothes that need refreshening. You can wash most clothes with just warm water or a small amount of soap. Your skin will thank you for using fewer chemicals—and so will the groundwater! While you're at it, eliminate dryer additives that purport to soften clothes. Less detergent can achieve the same results. *Buy and store fewer products.*

❏ **Designate a bag or basket for delicates.**
Create a simple place for stockings, lingerie, blouses, and sweaters that must be washed by hand or on the delicate cycle.

❏ **Plan a Clothes Swap!**
Wearing new fashions is fun, but paying off credit cards isn't. Instead of buying new clothes, invite people over for a Clothes Swap. Tell each person to bring a pile of giveaways and an appetizer, and you provide the drinks.

❏ **Create a Clothing Repair Center.**
Hang clothing that needs a button, mending, or altering away from your wearable garments. If possible, do all of your mending in one sitting. Or take them to a seamstress and save time.

❏ **Repair your shoes in one trip.**
On your calendar, mark a day every six months for getting *all of your shoes* tapped, heeled, and polished. Be proactive. Avoid emergency trips to the cobbler. As your life becomes simpler, you will want to own fewer pairs of shoes and you will wear them longer.

❏ **Keep a Recycle Bag in your closet.**
Create a convenient place to collect an old shirt, a tight skirt,

and an outdated suit. This eliminates having giveaways sit in the hallway or on a bedroom chair.

❏ Create an Ambivalence Center.
Put your ambivalent clothing—*clothing you can't get rid of but don't really like*—away from clothing you frequently wear. Put these items in the back of your closet, in another closet, in an under-the-bed box, or in your garage in stacked, lidded boxes. After a few months, try on these clothes to see how you feel about them. You may like some items better, and want them back in your closet—and you may like some less, and want to discard them.

❏ Try the Out-of-Sight Box.
Confronting a jam-packed closet can be confusing. Why not gather up a third to a half of your clothes—*garments you like, not ambivalent items*—and store them, out of sight, in a box or in another closet. Then, in six months, trade these clothes for items in your closet. You will feel like you have a new wardrobe.

❏ For Serious Simplifiers only!
Design a highly organized closet *immediately*. To become inspired, visit closet companies and stores like Hold Everything and Stacks & Stacks. Make your hangers one kind and one color. Next, radically pare down your wardrobe. Recycle at least half of your clothing and accessories. Put your clothes back into your closet using a simple arrangement. (See "Arrange your clothing inventively" above.) Finally, remove your shoes from the closet floor and restrict them to neutral colors. After seven days, review your closet and work out the bugs!

∽

Anyone who has ever cleaned out a closet and taken stuff to Goodwill knows how liberating it is. You feel lighter, your mind feels clearer.

—Cecile Andrews, author of *The Circle of Simplicity*

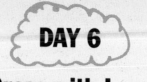

DAY 6

Dress with Less

Task: *Spend at least an hour reviewing your wardrobe. Create a wardrobe without "strays"—items that don't go with anything else. Identify your strays and hang them at one end of your closet. Plan to buy something to go with them or give them away!*

When did you lose control of your closet? Perhaps you lost it when you were a teenager, when clothes and boys became more important than grades.

Connie will never forget the eighth grade, the year her wardrobe became the center of her life. She remembers standing in front of her closet every morning, moaning about what to wear. She also remembers discovering that her body was not perfect. She was a teenager with all of the trappings.

"I was distraught before the day began," she says. "Then we moved to Norway. For six chilly months, my parents, brother, sister, and I lived in the village of Horten in a one-bedroom up-stairs flat heated with a coal stove. My siblings and I slept in the bedroom on cots. Our suitcases became dressers.

"My parents slept in the dining room, which was separated from the living room by a curtain. The bathroom was in an un-heated hall and hot water was available for one bath every twelve hours. *Life was simple.*

"At school, I quickly made friends, and Kirsti became my best friend. After a while, I realized that she owned just two pairs of slacks for winter, a charcoal pair and a brown pair. Both were durable, well made, and attractive. Kirsti also had a dark green V-neck sweater, a great-looking Norwegian ski sweater, a navy crew neck, a pleated skirt that she wore for special occasions, and a handsome car coat that she wore every day, everywhere. That was her entire winter wardrobe.

"I realized that all of the girls in the class dealt with their clothes in a similar manner. Each had what I call 'signature clothes,' or a personal style. They seldom thought about clothes. It was not their reason for being. I grew to admire them because, unlike my American peers, they spent little time shopping for clothes or agonizing over what to wear. Instead, they spent time knitting, cooking, eating, going to the movies, cross-country skiing, and hiking all over town to visit friends.

"Being an impressionable thirteen-year-old, I imitated my new friends' fashion philosophy. I owned a black pair of wool pants, a favorite pair of jeans, a red sweater and, of course, a Norwegian sweater. Also, like them, I had a pleated skirt—mine was black and red. Every day, I walked to school in the same boots and wore a pair of tennis shoes at home. Dressing like a Norwegian schoolgirl was easy. I felt comfortable and free of worry.

"Six months passed quickly and soon I was back in high school in Southern California. Being back felt strange. I felt an undefined anxiety and *I quickly acculturated*. Once again, I assumed I needed a large wardrobe, agonized over what to wear, and criticized my body. I truly believed that more was better. As I have gotten older, I realize how freeing it is to have fewer clothes."

European Women Dress with Less

European women have fewer clothes than we do. But they spend more money on each garment. We spend less on each item and buy much, much more. They are more interested in quality; we are interested in quantity. We have bigger closets; they have smaller closets.

Looking unique is second nature on the Continent. Before going out, women seldom consult one another. They rarely ask "What are you going to wear?" Instead, they dress with a sense of humor and willingness to experiment, always with self-awareness. They mix separates in offbeat ways and know how to add accessories that dazzle.

And that's not all. European women know how to play up the best parts of their figures while many American women tend to focus more on disguising their flaws. To be more like European women, develop a personal style and stay with it.

Shop for Clothes Biannually

Many women don't have much time or energy to shop for clothes. So what's the solution? *Shop twice a year.* Once in the fall—for fall and winter clothes. And once in the spring—for spring and summer clothes.

At these times, buy the outfits you need including coordinating tops, pants, skirts, jackets, belts, shoes, scarves, purses, and stockings or socks. Keep from owning a closet full of mismatches.

When a great sale occurs or you are in a "shopping mood," you can add great pieces that enhance your basic wardrobe. To become a biannual shopper do the following:

- *Before you go shopping,* examine your wardrobe and recycle garments you rarely wear. If you are like most women, you have more clothes than *time* to wear them.
- *Next, make a list* of what you need in order to fully use what you have. Maybe you need a belt or a short-sleeved white top or pair of black flats to complement your wardrobe.
- *Finally, decide what you will need for the next season.* A new pantsuit with a couple of tops in the hot new colors? A pair of great looking shoes in a new style? A new pair of jeans? A sweater that will add sparkle to last year's fashions? If you stick with your list and shop all at once, every-

thing will go together. You will be ready for the coming season.

Shop Wisely

Create a simple, supportive, hassle-free wardrobe, one that reflects your personal style. When you shop, either create a complete outfit or buy a separate that goes with an outfit you already have.

When you shop for clothes choose . . .

- *multiseasonal clothes.* Look for clothes that may be worn year round, that may be dressed up or dressed down. "There's no longer such a thing as seasonal color," says Bill Blass. Nor is there a seasonal weight. For instance, a black lightweight wool suit is the most versatile basic you can own.
- *garments that layer well.* Think multifunctional! Pieces that layer enable you to have a wider variety of outfits. Also, layering allows you to adjust to temperature changes easily.
- *clothes with simple lines.* Choose styles that do not jolt the eye at every turn. Simplicity is elegant and timeless.
- *smooth fabrics over coarsely textured.* Smooth fabrics are more useful than nubby fabrics. They layer better, feel better, and project a look of simplicity and good taste.
- *plain clothes over prints.* Plain fabrics, which lend to unusual and interesting color combinations, are more versatile than printed fabrics.
- *quiet colors over loud.* Use brights sparingly. Save them for accent pieces.
- *classic over trendy.* Classic clothes are stylish—and you may wear them into the twenty-first century without dying of embarrassment.
- *machine washable fabrics.* To simplify, make fewer trips to the dry cleaners and toss out your iron. Our savvy friends iron only for meditative purposes.

- *clothes that travel well.* Look for clothes that can be folded, rolled, and stuffed into a suitcase and will bounce back looking terrific, not like the underside of a mushroom. We know a fashion consultant in Seattle who organizes wardrobes to fit into a duffel.

Fashion Simplifiers

Grace Mirabella says, "What I've always cared about, passionately, is style. Style is how a woman carries herself and approaches the world. It's about how she wears her clothes and it's more: It's an attitude about living."

Make a red check mark by tips that will simplify your wardrobe.

❏ **Wear comfortable clothing.**
Forget tight waistbands. Life is too short to be cinched in. Go for elasticized bands or loose waistbands that cinch up with a belt, even if you are thin. Pick clothing that lets you move freely and feels luxurious next to your skin. Cindy Crawford says, "I feel sexiest in clothes that are comfortable—my favorite jeans, cashmere sweaters, and silk nightgowns."

❏ **Own fewer accessories.**
Sort through your accessories—jewelry, scarves, belts, and bags—and delete items that no longer delight you. Keep a few pairs of great daytime earrings and a few for evening. Mixed gold and silver earrings can be worn with everything. Give all of those cutesy earrings you never wear to the girl next door. Kate wears the same thick gold hoops 365 days a year. For evenings out, she owns pearl studs the size of green peas. *Who is Kate?* She is the most simplified yet well-dressed woman we know.

❏ **Declutter your purse.**
An organized purse saves time. Think about the frantic moments you waste as you fumble for your keys, pens, money, and

lip balm. Take everything out of your handbag, toss as much as possible, and put back the essentials. Group similar things together in small zippered bags.

❑ **Carry a handbag with useful compartments.**
To simplify, carry a highly organized, lightweight handbag. Heavy shoulder bags can cause leg-length discrepancy and functional scoliosis. Here are three healthier choices:

- *The bag with an extra-long strap.* Wear this purse diagonally across your chest. By positioning the weight in front of your pelvis, you distribute the weight evenly and minimize torque. Look for wallet-styled purses with slots and pockets for everything.
- *The backpack purse.* Today many designers make handsome backpacks. Backpacks free up your arms to do other things.
- *The fanny pack.* Walk unencumbered with both arms swinging freely.

❑ **Own a few basic pairs of shoes.**
Be honest! You know you only wear some of your shoes, and you wear them most of the time. Put these favorites in the front part of your closet and see if you can get by with only these. Toss old sneakers. Eliminate as many frivolous, costume, special-use shoes as possible. They clutter your mind and your closet.

❑ **Get rid of shoes that hurt.**
Shoes that are too short or too narrow and can't be stretched need to be tossed. Your feet will not shrink. Next, rethink high heels. Forcing your toes to conform to a V shape while standing or walking on a slant is inhumane. Donna Karan says, "Who wears high heels every day? Is that modern? You can't get anywhere in them." Cybill Shepherd says, "The only place appropriate for five-inch heels is in bed!"

❑ **Look for naturally colored organic cotton clothing.**
Recently, we discovered that 25 percent of all insecticides used

worldwide are sprayed on cotton. The spraying kills birds, fish, wildlife, and beneficial insects, and contaminates groundwater. Here are some alternatives:

- *Green cotton:* Best choice. It is grown organically and is free of chemical dyes, bleaches, fungicide, and pesticides used on cotton during shipping and production.
- *Organic cotton:* Second best choice. It is not grown with pesticides, but is dyed with poisonous chemicals.

❏ For Serious Simplifiers only!

"Freeze your wardrobe," says Allison, an artist living in Boston. At first, we thought she was suggesting we put our clothes in cold storage. A shuddering thought! But she meant, "Don't buy any new clothes *for a specified time period*—freeze your wardrobe in its current state (and continue to cull out the clothes you rarely wear). When you feel compelled to buy something new, write it down on a list."

∽

Oh, how much money is spent on our bodies and how little upon our souls.

DAY 7

Transform Your Bathroom

Task: *Today, clear your bathroom counter of everything. Then add no more than three items. Good choices are a water glass, soap dish, and a scented candle. Next, declutter your bathroom cabinets and drawers. Toss any product in a jar, tube, or bottle that you have not used for six months. Include prescription and over-the-counter drugs, dried up hand cream, and perfume bottles that are so old the insides are dark brown. Bathrooms need not be a haven for half-used, nearly empty, never-to-be-opened containers.*

Imagine that you will be moving into a small condo two blocks from the beach and your new bathroom can only accommodate a quarter of your current bathroom products. With this scene in mind, do the above task.

As you look into your bathroom storage areas, find products you can comfortably eliminate. Recently, Cris decided she can live without eye cream, mouthwash, tissues, paper cups, and hair conditioners. Connie eliminated perfume, hair spray, and her shower cap!

Keep fewer bottles under the bathroom sink.

When streamlining the space under the sink, remember—all that is contrary to the essential must be relinquished. Delete, delete, delete. Create space around every item.

Today is also a good day for reviewing your towels and

washcloths. Determine precisely how many you need. Figure out the exact number for each family member. Two to four bath towels and four washcloths is ample for each person. Then keep a few hand towels for that towel ring next to the sink, a few for camping trips, and a few for rags. Send the rest to Old Towel Heaven.

People seldom take the time to calculate how many of anything they truly need—how many towels, washcloths, glasses, place mats, hangers, shoes, purses, and so on. Living simply is about making clear decisions about what is needed.

Bathroom Simplifiers

The word *purity* means clarity and cleanliness. It's the perfect word for describing a simplified bathroom.

Make a red check mark by tips that will simplify your bathroom.

❏ **Create a serene bathroom.**
Think of ways to make your bathroom more serene.

- Conceal your toothbrush, toothpaste, and floss. Do you really want to be reminded of dental plaque when you go into your bathroom?
- Place the trash basket under the sink. If you don't have a bathroom cabinet, get a trash can with a swing top. Soiled Q-tips, tissue, and cotton balls are unattractive to look at.
- Use tricks to make your bathroom seem larger: Install a large mirror. Hang a translucent shower curtain. Paint the ceiling a lighter color.
- Hang fewer tiny pictures and change flowery towels to plain.
- Clear off the windowsill and toilet tank lid.

❏ **Protect your body from chlorine.**
Chlorinated water is harmful to hair, skin, eyes, and lung and nose membranes. You take in more chlorine from one fifteen-

minute shower than from drinking eight glasses of the same water. Chlorine chemically bonds with the protein in our bodies. It makes your hair brittle and skin flaky. In addition, byproducts of chlorine have been linked to cancer. Shower filters remove about 90 percent of the chlorine from shower water. If you cannot find shower filters locally, call The Harmony catalogue at 1-800-456-1177. Filters make great shower gifts. (No pun intended!)

❏ **Install first-rate organizers.**
One of the rules of organizing is—*cluster similar objects*. To make your deep vanity shelves more useful and coherent, group objects on Lazy Susans or in attractive baskets. For bathroom drawers, use silverware trays or desk drawer dividers. One day, Cris spent two hours looking for the perfect basket for her makeup. Spend more time looking for top-notch organizers.

❏ **Hang your towels on hooks or extra-long bars.**
To hang towels, Connie uses large brass hooks mounted on wood. She says, "Towels draped over a large hook are easier to hang—and dry quickly." She also installs a strategically placed hook for a robe and clothing. Cris likes an extra-long 28-inch bar—the longest length made—because this size holds an unfolded towel.

❏ **Simplify your grooming ritual.**
Note what you use daily and create a precise routine.

• Stock each shelf and drawer with similar types of grooming products. For instance, put cleanser, toner, and face creams on a single shelf in your medicine cabinet. On the next shelf, put dental hygiene products.
• To simplify your makeup routine, place the products you use daily in a drawer or basket. Put your choices for other occasions elsewhere. *Spend less time dealing with choices.*

❏ **Keep your jewelry in a drawer.**
If you have an extra drawer in your bathroom, use it for your

everyday jewelry and watches. Padded lingerie dividers or kitchen drawer dividers will keep everything organized. It is convenient to put on jewelry after you put on makeup.

❏ **Try Cris's inclusive skin care line.**
Cris used to buy exclusive, overpackaged creams and lotions. Now she makes her own products from ingredients found in health food stores.

- *Face Cleanser:* Combine equal parts rosewater and vegetable glycerin.
- *Toner:* Make green tea with filtered water and spray it on your face (after it cools).
- *Moisturizer:* Use vegetable or fruit oils, like jojoba, apricot, and grapeseed oil. Put a few drops on wet skin. At night, let it soak in. For daytime, blot and then add makeup.
- *Hair conditioner:* A few drops of fruit or vegetable oil conditions dry hair.
- To explore natural skin care products further, read Stephanie Tourles's *The Herbal Body Book*. Natural skin care products make unique gifts.

❏ **Get a "wash 'n wear" haircut.**
Blow-drying is time consuming and dries out your hair. Invest in a haircut that looks great air-dried. If you prefer using a hair dryer, make it convenient to use. Connie has a blow-dryer drawer with an under-the-sink plug so it is always plugged in. She keeps a hairbrush in the same drawer.

❏ **Try the "Outdoor Clawfoot Hot Tub."**
If you like the idea of soaking in an outdoor hot tub, try the Outdoor Clawfoot Hot Tub—a two-person soaking tub with side-installed faucets. Find an old clawfoot tub for about $100, place it on your deck, and run hot and cold water pipes to it. After you soak, let the water trickle into your garden. Installing a clawfoot hot tub is easy and inexpensive. Also, it requires less maintenance than a commercial hot tub. Because it is empty

except when being used, there is no liability—i.e., no expensive insurance costs!

❑ Wash away your troubles in a tub full of bubbles.

Living simply is about creating simple pleasures, such as relaxing in a warm tub. "It's the one place I am not interrupted by phones, faxes, e-mail, and family members," says Connie. If you like to read while you soak, install excellent overhead lighting. Put your reading material in a basket and use it in your bedroom and bathroom. Keep recycling those magazines and catalogues!

❑ Get rid of nail polish.

You probably have enough nail polish to paint a car. Pick out a couple of colors that become you and get rid of the rest. Or better yet, stop wearing polish and buff your nails.

❑ For Serious Simplifiers only!

Think of the freedom you have when you travel with a makeup kit and a few toiletries. With that image in mind, remove *everything* from your bathroom counter, cabinets, and drawers. (Go for one brand of each item—you don't need three kinds of cold medicine.) After that, put back your essentials. Finally, hang plain-colored towels and eliminate excess wall art.

∽

A bathroom should be sterile and beautiful and functional. It should exude Japanese-style purity.

—Isaac Mizrahi, fashion designer

DAY 8

Streamline Your Kitchen

Task: *Take an hour to go through your pantry. Remove everything you will never get around to eating—like that candied fruit you received as a gift, that low-sodium soup that tastes awful, and those seasoning envelopes that are five years old. Then toss items with dates that have expired. Update your pantry today.*

While you are in the kitchen, take a few minutes to streamline your countertops. Remove everything you don't use daily. Be ruthless and uncompromising.

It makes sense to leave daily used items on your kitchen counters, such as a toaster or coffeemaker, but not rarely used items like stale spices, tiny potted plants, boring cookbooks, empty cookie jars, barren bread boxes, and souvenirs from your trip to Turkey in the seventies. Also, dump that freestanding paper towel holder (hang your towels) and that knife block (store your knives in a drawer). Put away the seldom used bread machine and the standing mixer. Keep your kitchen counters clear so they will always be ready for what they are meant for—preparing food!

Look Under the Sink

Remove everything from the cabinet beneath your kitchen sink. Bottles of many shapes and sizes lurk there: bottles of flea powder, plant fertilizer, spot remover, oven cleaner, and dish-washing liquid. So do old rags, sponges, brushes, and scrubbies. Once you have removed everything, clean the cupboard and organize it.

Lazy Susans work especially well under kitchen sinks.

As you put each item back, ask yourself, "How often do I use it?" and "Does this really belong here?" Toss anything you have not used in six months. Combine bottles of like products. Reduce the amount of stuff under your sink. The more space you have between items, the easier it is to retrieve them.

Our friend Annie doesn't like to bend over to retrieve under-the-sink cleaning supplies, so she puts them in an upper cabinet. She says, "I like having nothing but the trash basket under the sink."

Come up with offbeat solutions to make life easier.

Kitchen Simplifiers

Think about how you use your kitchen. In addition to storing, preparing, and cooking food, many people use their kitchen as a command center for mail, phones, messages, and paperwork. Others use it as a place to gather with friends and family. Make a mental list of your kitchen activities. Is its arrangement supportive of what you wish to accomplish? If not, what can you do to make your kitchen more user-friendly?

Make a red check mark by tips that will simplify your kitchen.

❑ **Control your cupboards.**
Your kitchen cupboards are high-use spaces. They are not spaces for storing infrequently used items. Organize all of these cupboards so you can quickly find the things you need.

- *Create space around the items in your cupboards.* If you do not have space around stored items, you have too much stuff. Edit, edit, edit.

- *Put your least-used items on hard-to-reach shelves.* Analyze the location of every item in your cupboards. Ask yourself, "Is it too far away?" or "Does it have to be so close at hand?"
- *Decide how many glasses and mugs you need for daily use.* Store your glasses for entertaining in a less convenient location. We have found that a set of matching mugs is more soothing to the eye than a collection of mismatched mugs of many sizes, shapes, and colors. Also, having complete sets of glasses is an inexpensive way to bring order into your life.

❏ **Edit your kitchen drawers.**

Drawers are valuable spaces because they can be reached easily. Save them for items you use frequently.

- *Get rid of utensils you have not used in six months.* Yes, that could mean an egg beater and a potato masher. We don't need a special tool for every purpose. Store rarely used utensils in a shoe box on a top shelf—call it your Ambivalent Utensils Box.
- *Create a drawerful of cloth napkins.* Cloth napkins are practical, attractive, and eco-friendly. Buy napkins that don't need ironing and use them lavishly. To reuse napkins and remember to whom they belong, use personalized napkin rings or give each person his own color. Terry cloth hand towels make super everyday napkins.

❏ **Take charge of your fridge.**

- *Clean out your fridge weekly.* A crammed fridge is a sign of a complicated life. Get rid of those half-filled bottles of barbeque sauce, nearly empty salad dressings, and tired leftovers. Notice how good it feels to have an updated fridge.
- *Fill your freezer with water bottles to make it run more efficiently.* Empty freezers cost more to run. Every time you empty a large water bottle, fill it with filtered water and

put it in the freezer until it is frozen. (If there is an earthquake, you will be prepared.)

- *Minimize refrigerator magnets.* Magnets are visually distracting. The fewer, the better. Install a giant bulletin board for kids' art.

❏ **Manage your kitchen appliances.**

- *Get rid of all of the appliances you have not used in a year.* Do you use that hot dog cooker, electric knife, or antique waffle iron? If not, recycle these items.
- *Round up your appliance manuals.* Include booklets for the stove, microwave, refrigerator, freezer, toaster, disposal, washer, dryer, juicer, coffee makers, and so on. Toss the ones of no value, like a warranty on a three-year-old juicer. Put your needed warranties in a kitchen drawer. Or create a file called Kitchen Appliances. Write the date and place of purchase on the front of each manual.

❏ **Set up a message/mail center.**
If your kitchen is the center of life in your house, set up a command center.

- *Make a phone binder:* Make a binder with sheets containing useful information—rosters, phone numbers, schedules, emergency numbers, household instructions, take-out menus, and a calendar for the whole family. This binder can eliminate a drawer full of pieces of paper. Reduce the complexity!
- *Create a mail system:* Use stacking In and Out trays for family mail. Provide a tray for each member. This tray can also be used for phone messages, permission slips, and kids' library books to be returned. One upright file folder per person works as well.

❏ **Find a great dispenser for dishwashing liquid.**
Don't waste time reaching under the sink every time you need soap for washing dishes. Fill an attractive plastic squeeze bottle

and set it beside the sink. Try a Honey Bear bottle. Ceramic pump bottles are good choices, too.

❑ Clear your kitchen windowsills.
Is your view of the natural world obscured by windowsill ornaments—figurines, tiny cacti, vitamin bottles?

❑ Consider a television in the kitchen.
If working in the kitchen feels like a waste of time, put a small TV on a counter or, even better, on a shelf. Catch the news while chopping or cleaning up. Our friend Eileen has a small TV with a built-in VCR. She often watches old movies or documentaries while she is working in the kitchen.

❑ For Serious Simplifiers only!
Imagine that you are going to paint the inside of your cupboards and drawers white. To get ready for the painter, box up everything in your kitchen. *Do that today. Haul everything out to the garage.* Then, after the imaginary paint dries, bring back what you need—as you need it. After six months, recycle everything you didn't use.

∽

Modern life is becoming so full that we need our own ways of going to the desert to be relieved of our plenty.

—Thomas Moore

DAY 9

Fix Quick and Healthy Meals

Task: *Organize your recipes! Make a three-ring binder for Favorite Family Recipes and another for Recipes to Try. You will need two binders, two divider sets with tabs, a three-hole punch, and a few clear vinyl sheet protector pages.*

Notebook #1. Favorite Family Recipes: Gather all of your recipe cards, recipes from magazines, and your favorite dog-eared recipes in cookbooks. On 8 1/2 x 11–inch paper, photocopy recipes you use frequently. Divide them into hors d'oeuvres, salads, entrées, and desserts. Place them into your notebook. This notebook will contain all those old favorites like Mom's Apple Crisp and Uncle Charlie's Chili. It will not contain untried recipes.

Notebook #2. Recipes to Try: Create another binder with dividers and add a top-loading clear sheet protector to each section. Recipes collected from magazines and friends are placed inside the sheet protectors. When you have several odd sizes collected, photocopy them onto 8 1/2 x 11–inch paper, punch, and put into the notebook. After you have tried a recipe from this notebook, and know it is a keeper, transfer it to your Favorite Family Recipes notebook.

The Favorite Family Recipes notebook is designed to help you collect recipes you have enjoyed over the years, recipes you will use often. By keeping it handy, you will always know where to go for ideas when you are pressed for time, or when you are not feeling particularly creative.

The Recipes to Try notebook is designed to eliminate the clutter of clipped recipes stuck in drawers or on shelves around the kitchen.

Next, ruthlessly survey your cookbooks. Get rid of the ones you haven't opened in ten years—perhaps that one on soufflés or barbecuing or cake decorating. Many older cookbooks are filled with recipes that are deemed unhealthy today. Fattening desserts, gravies, and meat dishes are not as popular as they used to be. Get rid of those, too. While writing this book, we recycled more than half of our cookbooks.

Simplicity means having a few favorite cookbooks.

Simplify Everyday Eating

Everyday meals can be made without complicated recipes. Multiple-ingredient sauces are optional. To simplify, create simple meals with few ingredients at home and enjoy complicated meals when you dine out. Or wait for the weekend, when you might have more time.

In almost every one of Connie's workshops, a woman raises her hand and says, "When my husband is out of town, I enjoy ordering pizza and making a salad for myself and the kids. I do less." Connie replies, "I recommend you do less when he's in town."

We believe that families eating dinner together in a relaxed atmosphere with good conversation is more important than cooking complicated dinners from scratch and striving for the Good Housekeeping Seal of Approval. Dinner can be a piece of baked chicken, a vegetable, and French bread. Or grab a deli entrée and serve it with a dish of fresh tomatoes sprinkled with parsley. Our goal is to simplify meal preparation, serve healthy meals, make each meal appealing, and enjoy the company of the people with whom we share our meals.

Make a red check mark by tips that will simplify everyday eating.

❏ **Create simple grain-and-veggie medleys.**
Stir-fry veggies into cooked grains such as brown rice, couscous, bulgur wheat, buckwheat, quinoa, and pastas. Couscous cooks in five minutes. Bulgur wheat can be soaked for about 3 hours. Make a list of your favorite grain medleys for your Favorite Recipes notebook. Toss grains with:

- Salsa and a can of drained black beans.
- Olives, feta, tomatoes, and a green vegetable.
- Chicken, broccoli, garlic, and green onions.
- Corn kernels, green onions, red bell peppers, toasted sesame seeds, roasted cashews, a little canola oil, soy sauce, and rice wine vinegar. Outstanding!

❏ **Create salad entrees.**
A hearty salad can be dinner. Top salads with:

- Roasted beets and/or potatoes.
- Steamed broccoli, asparagus, or green beans.
- Cold cooked grains such as rice, quinoa, couscous, and bulgur wheat.
- A mound of tuna, cottage cheese, cubed tofu, or stir-fried chicken.
- Bread slathered with warm goat cheese.

❏ **Get more protein from beans.**
Simplicity and beans make a great team. Eat beans at least twice a week. Make bean soups. Add beans to grain medleys. Put beans in your tacos and enchiladas. Experiment with different varieties. Enjoy bean cuisine.

❏ **Try a rice cooker.**
People who have rice cookers rave about them. Rice cookers make it easy to have fresh, warm rice for dinner. Try leftover rice for breakfast, heated in the microwave, with raisins, brown sugar, banana slices, and milk.

❏ **Soak grain flakes for breakfast.**

To make a delicious breakfast cereal, soak one or more kinds of bulk grain flakes overnight in a small lidded casserole dish, in equal parts milk and water. Add liquid an inch above the flakes. To sweeten, add raisins or honey. Make a combo out of oat, rye, and barley flakes. Be adventuresome and add spelt or kamut flakes.

Simplify Having Friends for Dinner

Do you wish you could have friends over more often? Do you hesitate to invite them because it's such a hassle? If so, you are not alone. Meeting friends at a restaurant seems to be the norm these days. But this was not always the case.

In the seventies, having people over was fun because dinners were simple. People loved coming over for spaghetti, a salad, and garlic bread. In the eighties, things got complicated. It was not unusual for a busy woman to spend all day preparing for guests. Dinner and entertaining became such an ordeal that today we may be experiencing a backlash.

In the nineties, we are making dinner with friends enjoyable again. Meals are easier to prepare. The formal has been replaced by the informal. Our mantra is *relax and enjoy it.*

How we complicated it!

- *Elaborate table settings:* Presenting the right centerpiece, candles, tablecloth and napkins, dishes, glasses, and silverware can be daunting. To simplify, get one set of everything for eight people and use it over and over again. As you entertain more, create variations.
- *Multi-course dinners:* It can take hours to prepare hors d'oeuvres, soup, salad, a main course, and dessert. You don't have to compete with four-star restaurants. A dinner of broiled halibut, a salad, and fresh berries for dessert is simple and lovely. Gourmet takeout is a wonderful option.
- *Worrying about whether your house is pulled together:* You might think your house isn't clean enough, orderly enough, or attractive enough. Friends are less concerned

with appearances than you may imagine. On the other hand, you might invite people to dinner as an incentive to finish things you have been putting off for months, such as throwing away a straggly plant, rearranging the living room, or repainting the front door.

How to simplify it!

- *Ask guests to bring a dish.* Make an entrée, like fish or pasta, and ask your guests to bring a salad or dessert. If your friends are busy, they can pick up a dish at a deli or bring salad ingredients and assemble them at your house.
- *Invite guests for coffee, tea, and dessert.* Dessert nights lend themselves to entertainment. Play board games. Show your latest vacation photos. Watch a television special, such as the Academy Awards.
- *Prepare simple hors d'oeuvres and repeat them.* Connie frequently serves hummus with toasted pita bread, or Brie with crackers accompanied by a bunch of grapes. Cris often serves blue corn chips with salsa, guacamole, and warm refried beans.
- *Put a tablecloth on your coffee table.* Set your coffee table with a red-checkered tablecloth, two votive candles, and a petite vase of flowers. Sit on the floor and enjoy a simple dinner.
- *Use votive candles.* Votive candles in clear glass cups don't topple or interfere with centerpieces. Put them on the dining table and dot them around on tables, counters, and bookshelves. Put 1/4 inch of water in the bottom of the cup to make the wax easier to remove. Try votives made of beeswax—paraffin is a petroleum derivative.

Create several Guest Menus

Create a few one-page Guest Menus. Call each menu by a number and/or a name such as The Greek Pasta Dinner or The Salmon and Wild Rice Dinner. Place your menus in the back section of your Favorite Family Recipes notebook. Make several copies of each menu. Use them for buying groceries on your way home from work. On each page, include:

- *The Menu:* The food and beverages. The hors d'oeuvres, salad, soup, main dish, side dishes, dessert, and drinks.
- *Grocery List:* The ingredients.
- *Instructions for Preparation:* A quick description for preparing each dish. These notes are for you. You are not writing a cookbook.

When you use your Guest Menu sheet, notes and substitutions may be added. For example, you might want to substitute fresh asparagus for broccoli or a take-out pasta sauce for the one you normally make. Connie went to a dinner party where the hostess leaned over to her husband, after hearing him rave about the food, and said, "By the way, you're eating dinner number eighteen!" She does lots of corporate entertaining in her home.

On a separate sheet, list what you need for a dinner party.

- *Have Ready:* This list includes cocktail napkins, glasses, hors d'oeuvres platters, place settings (dishes, silverware, serving pieces), flowers, and candles.
- *Do Ahead:* Your list might include things like: (1) Put candles and clean hand towels in the bathroom; check the toilet paper. (2) Rent a video for the kids. (3) Put flowers in the living room.

The Simplicity Diet

There's the Zone Diet, the Food Combining Diet, the Blood-Type Diet, and the Brain Longevity Diet. And what if each family member has a different diet? We empathize. We think the healthiest meals contain the fewest ingredients, eaten raw, steamed, or stir-fried. What follows are five rules for healthy eating—but before changing your diet drastically, consult your family doctor:

Rule 1: Aim for a 50 percent raw diet

Eating more raw food means spending less time in the kitchen. We are the only animals who cook their food. The more you move toward a diet of uncooked food, the more healthy and vigorous you will be since practically all enzymes die at temperatures between 118 and 160 degrees. *Put living cells into your living body.*

Rule 2: Consume fewer faux foods

To be healthy, eat fewer bogus, pseudo, and fabricated foods. (Yes, like chemically flavored chips, sugary breakfast cereals, and fruit juice with just a trace of juice.) Avoid food with glitzy packaging, added vitamins and minerals, and words like "natural" and "low-fat" and "enriched." These foods are good for business, but not for your body.

Rule 3: Drink fruit and vegetable waters

Most of us walk around mildly dehydrated. Studies show that water deficits of as little as a quart can cause a decrease in mental and physical performance. So how can you get eight glasses of water a day? Drinking water can be boring. Try produce-flavored waters. Blend one peeled organic fruit or vegetable in eight ounces of filtered water. Try melons, pears, peaches, tomatoes, and cucumbers. These waters are much healthier than bottled juices, which contain fewer nutrients and more calories.

Rule 4: Drop sugar

Sugar suppresses your immune system. Sugar produces a significant rise in your triglycerides. Sugar makes you feel jittery. To be healthier, radically reduce your intake of sugar and sugar-related products—sucrose, fructose, corn syrup, and barley malt. According to Dr. Nancy Appleton, the author of *Lick the Sugar Habit*, there are 59 reasons to drop sugar.

Rule 5: Do One-Day Cleanses

You have probably heard how juice fasts and detox diets purify our bodies. Try the One-Day Cleanse. Spend one day, weekly or monthly, drinking fruit and vegetable juices that are freshly made. Fresh juices make your skin glow, eyes brighten, and hair shine.

Meal-Prepping Simplifiers

Simplify meal planning so that you will have more time to prep fresh vegetables and will be less tempted to buy packaged foods. Remember, fresh food has enzymes that are vital for all of your bodily processes.

Make a red check mark by tips that will simplify meals.

❏ **Streamline grocery shopping.**
The average American spends six hours a week shopping. Here are some ways to shorten this time.

- Print out a computer checklist for grocery basics.
- Keep a grocery pad in the kitchen to record family members' requests.
- Schedule a weekly trip to the farmer's market.
- Order groceries on-line. (Read about Peapod in Day 19.)
- Grow a garden full of veggies.

❏ **Simplify dinner with seven theme nights.**
Make a list of the days of the week. Beside each day, write a type of meal. For example, "Monday—Italian Night," "Tuesday—Mexican Night," and "Wednesday—Soup & Salad Night." Post the list and use it as a guide. *Rituals simplify life* and need not be boring. Each theme can have a dozen variations.

❏ **Prepare more back-to-back meals.**
Use *some* of the same ingredients for two dinners in a row. Make enough rice for two dinners. On the first night, make a rice stir-fry. On the second, make rice and bean enchiladas. Create a list of back-to-back meals.

❏ **Cook super quantities on Sundays.**
On Sundays, cook larger quantities than usual and freeze the excess. During the winter months, freeze soups in one-meal sizes. Serve them with a salad and you'll have a meal.

❏ **Simplify your herbs and spices.**
In one fell swoop, toss your stale seasonings. Wash out the jars and refill them, *as needed,* with bulk herbs and spices from your health food store. Alphabetize the jars to make hunting for the right spice easier.

❏ **Take home toppings from your grocery store salad bar.**
Let your local market wash, chop, and store a variety of vegetables for you. Buy just what you need and add the toppings to lettuce at home.

❏ **Make a binder or folder full of take-out menus.**
Use a three-ring binder or folder with pockets for your favorite take-out menus. Pamela keeps hers in a manila envelope.

❏ **Check out *The Kitchen Link,* a website for recipes.**
Betsey Couch's site (www.kitchenlink.com) has a comprehensive listing of recipes and food-related information. Type in an entree and receive links to other sites. You won't have to thumb through a pile of cookbooks. Cris typed in "peanut soup" and got a dozen recipes. The printed recipes went into her Recipes to Try binder.

❏ **For Serious Simplifiers only!**
Make a list of your top twenty simplest dinners. Select dinners with the fewest ingredients. Choose recipes with five or fewer ingredients. Post this list on your fridge and use it to plan dinners during the work week.

❧

Living simply is the best revenge.

DAY 10

Revise Your Living Spaces

Task: *Beware of overfurnished, overdecorated living spaces. Create feelings of comfort and serenity by living with less. Today, let go of at least ten knickknacks. There are three categories of knickknacks—meaningful, semimeaningful, and meaningless. Look for ones you have outgrown. If you can't part with ten, or any at all, put several in a cardboard box and store them out of sight, in an Ambivalence Center. Experience your home with fewer visual distractions.*

Cris is knickknack free. Her friends call her knickknack challenged. Actually, there is one tchotchke in her home, a model of a silver Porsche boxter, which belongs to her husband, Dave.

Sometimes people tell Cris that her version of simplicity is too monastic, Spartan, or Thoreauvian. Cris replies, "I want to become even less materialistic. I want to be surrounded by impermanence—like changing wall art and vases of fresh flowers. Knickknacks don't self-destruct fast enough for my taste."

Yes, Cris is a tchotchke-phobe.

Connie is more flexible about her home's decor. She enjoys displaying framed pictures and hand-painted Italian dishes, which Cris considers knickknacks.

If you are serious about simplifying your life, trade in your knickknacks for these substitutes:

Wall art. Objects on walls require less maintenance than knickknacks. But don't fill every wall. Leave some psychic breathing space.

A photo wall. Hang photos of your friends, relatives, favorite parties, and trips to foreign lands. Leave tables uncluttered by picture frames.

Practical souvenirs. A French cutlery tray, an English mug, lace curtains from Holland, and a T-shirt from Bakersfield are useful souvenirs.

Impermanent accessories. Fresh flowers and attractive candles are lovely today and gone tomorrow.

A grouping of small items. If you have a favorite collection, consolidate it in one place. Its impact will be greater than if you dot it around the house. Simplify.

The philosopher Gabriel Fielding said, "I'd like to become less acquisitive altogether, to be able to see some exquisite piece of porcelain in some other person's house and be wholly glad it was there—and not in mine."

The Rules for Simplified Living Spaces

Follow these rules and your rooms will be easier to manage and create a more tranquil backdrop for your busy life.

- *Choose large furniture over small.* A few large pieces of furniture are better than several small pieces. Large art objects are also preferable.
- *Install built-in cabinets with doors and drawers.* Built-ins are great for books, televisions, stereos, CDs, tapes, games, and candlesticks. Drawers of varying depths with dividers are available.
- *Don't go lamp crazy.* Consider overhead lighting or sconces with ambient lighting. Fewer table lamps mean fewer tables. Consider floor lamps, which take up very little space.
- *Avoid small pillows.* Sofa pillows added as accents can be

nuisances. They get pushed from one end of the sofa to another by those seeking a comfortable spot.

- *Beware of prints.* Printed fabrics and wallpapers can disrupt a room's sense of serenity. Choose tranquil prints or none at all.
- *Go for comfort.* All you really need in your living room is a comfortable sofa, a foot- and food-friendly coffee table, an ergonomic reading chair, good lighting, and one large plant.

Make Small Rooms Look Larger

Small homes have many advantages over large homes: There is less space to manage. Utility bills and property taxes are less. They are cozy and intimate. Succeeding with a small house depends on making it feel like a large one. Here are some ways to make small rooms appear larger.

- Remove doors that are seldom closed.
- Mount lamps on walls to avoid small tables.
- Install skylights and wall-sized mirrors to deepen space.
- Install floor-to-ceiling shelves in a living room or home office.
- Choose furniture with simple lines.
- Display few art objects.
- Install a scenic mural.

Tip: In a growing number of homes, murals and faux painting are being featured to brighten up drab hallways and add architectural interest to boring rooms. With murals, you can create illusions of space and graphically express your dreams.

Living in small spaces is not about sacrificing style.

Living Space Simplifiers

Using formulas from the past for designing and decorating homes can make life today unnecessarily complicated. Life was different then. Your mother or grandmother probably didn't have a demanding career. They may have had more kids, but after school their kids played with the kids on the block and weren't driven all over town to numerous extracurricular activities in a minivan.

Make a red check mark by tips that will simplify your living spaces.

❏ **Screen out distractions with standing screens.**
Freestanding screens are back in style. A screen can hide clutter, absorb sound, shade a window, create a cozy corner for privacy, and supply a dramatic focal point. Screens can be made of wood, rattan, metal, leather, and fabric that absorbs sound. Cris's favorite screen is louvered and painted the color of her walls. Screens fitted with photo frames are available and create a moveable gallery.

❏ **Consider natural fiber carpets.**
Today 97 percent of all carpets are made with synthetic fibers, and the gases from these fibers—such as benzene, formaldehyde, and xylene—can make you ill. The greatest quantities of gases are emitted in the first five years. Ideally, choose carpets made from nontoxic cotton or wool.

❏ **Use Feng Shui to create serenity.**
Feng Shui (pronounced fung shway) was conceived centuries ago. It evolved from the simple observation that people are affected, for good and for ill, by their surroundings—the layout and orientation of homes and workplaces. The goal of Feng Shui is to build environments in which we feel supported and at peace. For example, furniture should be placed so that, when you are seated, you can see who comes into the room. Feng Shui is gaining in popularity because, as the world becomes more complex, we have a greater need to retreat to a serene environment. A wonderful way to explore Feng Shui is to read Sarah Rossbach's book, *Interior Design with Feng Shui*. Learn the basics and apply them to your home.

❏ Reduce the noise in your home.

When people traipse through your house, does each footstep claim your attention? Does the television blast through the entire house? Think of ways to muffle noise. Carpets, baskets, and plants absorb sound. How about headphones for family members whose stereo and television habits are disturbing?

❏ Use baskets to simplify life.

Baskets allow you to group similar things together. Square and rectangular baskets work best for papers and magazines. Baskets whose dimensions are 3 x 11 x 14 inches keep papers together on tables, counters, and next to the phone. Baskets are light, durable, portable, and beautiful.

❏ Reduce your plant inventory.

Life inside a greenhouse can be complicated to maintain, depending on the number of plants. To simplify your living spaces, own a few large plants rather than a forest of small and medium-sized ones.

❏ For Serious Simplifiers only!

Abide by this rule: When something new comes into your home, let go of something old. Everything has a life cycle. Embrace change.

∽

Let every moment carry away all that it brought.

—André Gide

DAY 11

Consider Minimalism

Task: *Today, create a minimalist environment in one room. In that room, remove the wall art. (You might put it under the bed temporarily.) Next, remove everything except the lamps from tabletops, dressers, and counters. Most people live in rooms that are overfurnished and overstimulating. In these spaces, we are distracted from the present moment by too many objects from the past. This task will enable you to experience one extremely simplified room.*

Diane Wagner, the owner of three boutiques in Texas, did the task above and told us: "I created a bare-bones living room and like how peaceful it feels after a hectic day at work."

Terry Chambers, a contractor, had a similar experience. He radically simplified his den. "I removed all of my wall art except one large painting of the sea. I removed my black, red, and orange area rug. I can now think more clearly in my sparsely decorated den."

Molly Heebner, a flight attendant, edited the decor of her entire studio apartment. "I don't do things halfway. I got rid of tables, lamps, sofa pillows, framed photos, plants, books, and knickknacks. At first, it seemed sacrilegious to eliminate those things. I thought they kept me grounded. But I find I feel more centered without so many reminders of the past intruding on my consciousness."

Cris is a big fan of minimalism, the low-maintenance style of interior design that has its roots in the International Style of the 1930s. She thinks minimalism is the decorating style for the 1990s because it works for busy people.

Walk through your home and note the visual stimuli in your surroundings. How much is there? How many rooms are over-stimulating? How many feel tranquil? If you live in visually chaotic spaces, *consider minimalism*.

Master Minimalism's Maxims

San Francisco designer Gary Hutton says, "Minimalism is a good way to start in your home—it can always be added to and warmed up." Minimalism urges you to:

- *Choose quality over quantity.* W. Somerset Maugham said, "It's a funny thing about life—if you refuse to accept anything but the best, you often get it." Instead of having several items in a room, feature a few well-chosen pieces that don't fight with one another for attention.
- *Allow form to follow function.* Every form reflects its use and is not garish or pretentious. Philosopher Emile Durkheim must have been a minimalist. He said, "All that is contrary to the essential must be relinquished." Simple shapes are always the most refined and elegant.
- *Leave empty spaces.* Learn to see and feel empty spaces. "Don't feel compelled to fill up all the spaces in your home. Space is a luxury and having pure space will give you a serene feeling," says Susan Smith Jones in her book *Choose to Live Each Day Fully*.
- *Make comfort a prime consideration.* Many people think a sparsely decorated home is cool and uninviting. It doesn't have to be. Warmth may be achieved through the creative use of color, lighting, textures, and comfortable furnishings.

Become Surface Conscious

Flat surfaces breed dust and clutter. By "flat surfaces" we mean coffee tables, dining tables, bedside tables, hall tables, and behind-the-sofa tables, as well as fireplace mantels, windowsills, bureau tops, countertops, desktops, and heaters, refrigerators, speakers, televisions, and wall units. Floors create the greatest amount of horizontal space.

To radically simplify your life, eliminate as many flat surfaces as possible and keep the rest clear. Start with the ones you are the least attached to. You might let go of a spindly table that you bought at a flea market. Here are Cris's thoughts about the various surfaces:

- A coffee table is a necessity because it is useful for holding snacks, drinks, books, magazines, candles, and flowers. And feet!
- A dining table is a necessity. Keep it clear and ready for meals.
- Bedroom dressers are optional. Clothing can be stored in built-in closets.
- Sofa tables are optional. Wall lamps and track lighting are alternatives to table lamps.
- Kitchen countertops are necessary surfaces. Keep them cleared.
- Refrigerator tops tend to collect clutter. Keep a medium-sized plant on top of the fridge to discourage other items.
- Windowsills attract objects like magnets. Beware.

Minimalism and clutter don't mix. To achieve this style— *undecorate.*

The White Choice

Imagine peering into a white living room with white walls, white floors, and white furnishings. In front of the white sofa, there is a white coffee table with a white vase. In the vase is a flower. *A single yellow rose.*

Several years ago, Cris saw a photograph of a room like we have just described. She will never forget the yellow rose, the room's focal point. A year later, she wrote *How to Organize Your Closet . . . and Your Life!*, which had a cover photo of a white closet with white tubular hangers.

Color trends come and go, and of all the colors used in interior design, white is the favorite. White will never become trite, obsolete, or old-fashioned. In its countless shades, it is a classic. According to Benjamin Moore, a manufacturer of paints, 55 percent of its business is in whites.

Why does white endure?

White is calming. It's a soothing antidote for a stressful life. When the sun comes into a room, white walls turn golden and change constantly as the sun moves across them. The play of the sun is comforting.

White makes rooms seem larger than they are. A modest space feels spacious. Wood floors look impressive next to creamy white walls. Finally, white creates a stage on which accessories can shine. Colorful prints and paintings are shown off against a white background.

When choosing white for your home, consider exposure. For a north-facing room, use a warm white. For a south-facing room, use a cool white. Heighten ceilings with cool white. Learn to distinguish between the various shades of white by placing paint chips against the whitest piece of paper you can find.

For shimmer, glaze the walls in three shades of white, starting with the lightest underneath.

But isn't white impractical?

Not necessarily. For instance, you can slipcover a sofa or chair in an off-white canvas or cotton denim. Slipcovers are easy to clean and even bleachable. After reading the paragraphs above, Dave said, "I'm going to paint the inside of the garage white." He did and he loves it.

If white does not suit you, consider a monochromatic color scheme in which every room is a different value of the same hue, such as shades of gray, taupe, or sienna. Neutral does not have to be boring. Monochromatic palettes can be set off with white trim around doors, windows, and floors.

Minimalism's Simplifiers

Empty space is valuable. Life is movement, and space allows us to move freely. Appreciate the spaces in your life, and the feeling of moving easily through them.

Make a red check mark by tips that will simplify your home.

❏ **Go for oversized furniture.**
Oversized furniture tends to be more comfortable than standard and undersized. Also, rooms with a few large pieces appear more spacious than rooms with small sofas, chairs, and tables. Choose classic, straightforward pieces with simple silhouettes.

❏ **Display large art objects—not minuscule!**
Large vases, paintings, and sculptures are easier on the eye than a room full of small, fussy accessories. Limit medium-sized objects.

❏ **Avoid busy, patterned wallpaper.**
When you design a room around a dramatic pattern, you restrict the possibilities for *changing* and updating a room. If you want a lasting pattern, choose neutral designs.

❏ **Install more built-in cabinets.**
Use built-in cabinets for hiding all kinds of things—but don't let them become havens for clutter. Built-ins come with doors, drawers, and adjustable shelves. Use them in your den, living room, bedroom, bathroom, home office, and garage.

❏ **For Serious Simplifiers only!**
Create a minimalist environment in every room of your house. What more can we say?

∽

Less is more. —Ludwig Mies van der Rohe

DAY 12

Simplify Your Mind

Task: *Several years ago, we realized that the most cluttered area of our lives was our mind. We saw a direct link between a calm mind and a simple life. Today, you will do a task that teaches you how to clear your mind.*

First, you'll need a pen and a piece of paper.

Second, think of someone whose behavior makes you grumpy or angry. Anyone. It can be your spouse, child, parent, a friend, a co-worker, a neighbor, a company, or the government.

Third, fill in the blank in this sentence "_____ (name of the person) should/shouldn't _____ (write down the offensive behavior)." Be petty. The pettier you are, the better this task works. The task continues later.

Think of your mind as a lake that has the potential to be calm but is continually bombarded by millions of tiny pebbles causing so many ripples it cannot reflect reality. Think of the pebbles as *critical beliefs.*

Last year, we attended a workshop that profoundly affected our lives. It was about the nature of beliefs. The creator of the workshop, Byron Katie, has given us permission to share her realizations and techniques with you. Perhaps they will simplify your mind.

Realization 1: Beliefs and reality differ

Beliefs often describe how others *should behave*. Laura should be on time. Jenny should clean her room. Jason should apply to college. Bob should get a job. *Reality* describes how people *actually do behave*. Laura is rarely on time. Jenny's room is messy. Jason's college applications are not filled out. Bob is unemployed. Reality is what's happening. Beliefs are people's perceptions about reality.

Realization 2: Beliefs procreate like rabbits

There are two kinds of beliefs. First, a Primary Belief arises. For example, *Bonnie shouldn't smoke*. Then comes a barrage of Secondary Beliefs such as: She will get wrinkles. She will get cancer. People won't want to visit her. Nice men won't date her. Ad infinitum.

A *Belief System* is a cluster of beliefs—a Primary Belief and all of its babies, or Secondary Beliefs.

Realization 3: There are three kinds of business

Katie says there are three kinds of business—yours, other people's, and Nature's (or forces beyond your control). When you believe people should behave differently, you are in *their business*. "It's a terrific burden to be concerned about solutions to others' problems. One can significantly narrow down one's own suffering by restricting oneself to one's own business," writes Jack Dawson, a friend of Katie's. In other words, mind your own business.

Realization 4: Beliefs can cause stress

Task: *Now read the sentence you wrote. (If you didn't write it, do so now.) How does it make you feel? Look inside. Does it make you feel sad, upset, or anxious? Feel it. Take your time.*

You have just experienced, in a small way, what it feels like to have a critical thought about someone. Your thought destroyed your peace of mind. What a price to pay!

Realization 5: Critical beliefs diminish intimacy

Notice what happens to intimacy while you are thinking critical thoughts about someone—at lunch, on a walk, on the phone. A seemingly harmless thought like, "Her hair looks awful," can diminish intimacy. Such a thought leads to a stream of unconscious Secondary Beliefs such as—She has a bad perm. Her dye job is brassy. She obviously can't afford a good cut. Notice how hard it is to listen to someone while you are thinking they should change. Listening is hard work, even under the best of circumstances.

Realization 6: All beliefs are recycled

We are proud of our beliefs. We think they make us unique. But Katie says, "There are no original beliefs. They've all been recycled. Try to come up with a new one. I haven't heard one in ten years. It's no wonder we're bored—the same beliefs keep popping up. But who would you be without your beliefs? That's a scary thought for most people."

Realization 7: We know how to behave

"But without my beliefs, I won't know what to do." Don't worry, you'll know. When you get hungry, you'll eat. When you get tired, you'll sleep. When you get lonely, you'll call a friend. When your child misbehaves, you'll handle the situation. When there's a fire, you'll call 911.

Jon Kabat-Zinn, the author of *Wherever You Go There You Are*, says, "A non-judging orientation certainly does not mean that you cease knowing how to act or behave responsibly in society, or that anything anybody does is okay. It simply means that we can act with much greater clarity in our own lives, and be more balanced, more effective, and more ethical in our activities."

Katie's Two Techniques

You have gifts and possibilities you don't even know about because they are hidden under a mountain of beliefs. You often function below your level of potential because you are imprisoned by beliefs about yourself and others. Katie has come up with two techniques for letting go of burdensome beliefs as they arise.

Technique #1: Ask a question

When a Primary Belief, such as "She shouldn't stay with that loser," arises, *ask yourself* honestly, "Can I really know she shouldn't be with him?"

The answer is "No."

You can't know whether she should be with her mate. Why? Because you can't know what is best for another person—even if you have written a best-seller on codependent relationships.

We think we know what's best for our children, friends, neighbors, co-workers, parents, siblings, and the world. But most of the time we can't even know what is best for ourselves.

Saying "No" to a Primary Belief is a powerful act because it prevents a long train of Secondary Beliefs, such as: He is lazy. He is unfaithful. He is verbally abusive. He is mean to her children. She is wasting her time.

If you are attached to your statements about your friend's husband and you think, "But it's true. She should leave him," Katie would say, "I don't think so. She should be with him because she is. That's reality! A person's behavior is the result of many things—beliefs, attitudes, feelings, past experiences, heredity, and upbringing. You cannot know how the interplay of these factors works for or against others.

"Can you *want* your friend to leave her husband? Of course you can. *Wanting is not judging.* If you want something from others, just ask. You might say, 'Leave him for my sake. I'm concerned about your safety. I'll pay for you to spend two weeks in Hawaii in a hammock reading *The Givers and the Takers*. I'll take care of the kids.'

"The ball is now in her court. She may accept your kind offer to go to Hawaii. Or she may tell you it's none of your business. Or she may ask you if she and her five kids, two dogs, and three cats can move in with you. Since you cannot know how she will react, you may want to think twice before asking her to leave her husband."

Look at the belief you wrote down in the beginning. Now ask yourself, "Is it true? Can I really know how others should behave?" If you answered "No," the belief will disappear and so will your anger. If it reappears in the future, ask the question again. Soon the belief will disappear completely.

Technique #2: Reverse your beliefs

You know yourself in many ways—what foods you like, what music you enjoy, what kind of car you like to drive. But there is a way to know things that are less obvious. Subtle things.

To know yourself, reverse your judgments.

Beliefs are mirrors or projections. They are gifts from the universe. To receive your gifts, play with belief-reversals. Here's how to do it:

Substitute the pronoun "I" or the words "My mind," for the pronouns "She," "He," "They" in your judgments. For example, in the statement "She should stop smoking," say, "I should stop smoking." Isn't that also true? Isn't that your prescription for happiness? Your medicine?

Another reversal might be: "My mind is smoking with beliefs about my friend's habit" or "My stressful beliefs could give me cancer."

Try several reversals for each belief. Find the ones that resonate with you. Look for reversals that are as true or truer than the belief itself. Be creative with this process. Get to know yourself.

Here are two more examples of reversals. As you read them, notice how the judgment judges the judge.

EXAMPLE 1

Primary Belief: *My husband should remember to take out the trash.*

Secondary Beliefs: My husband isn't supportive. He's trying to frustrate me. He doesn't love me. Men do less housework than women.

Reverse it and know yourself: I am not a supportive wife. I am frustrating myself. I should love myself. If I feel resentful I should do less housework. My mind is full of garbage about my husband's behavior. Katie would add, "Reversing your judgments gently points the finger back at you, where you are in charge, where you can do something about the situation. It lets the other person off the hook. Look forward to beliefs arising, so you can know yourself. This is a belief's only purpose. Beliefs are friends, not enemies."

Reality: Your husband *shouldn't* take out the trash. How do you know that? He doesn't. That's reality. Accepting reality simplifies the mind. You can want him to take out the trash, and you can ask him to do it. He will or he won't. Don't become attached to the outcome.

The payoff for letting go of the belief: Clarity. Appropriate action.

EXAMPLE 2

Primary Belief: *People shouldn't pollute the planet.*

Secondary Beliefs: People don't recycle enough. People use too many toxic products. People don't think about global warming. People are cutting down too many trees.

Reverse it and know yourself: I should recycle more. I should use fewer toxic products. I should become more informed about global warming. I should plant trees. I should write a letter to my congressmen. I should drive my car less—or, better yet, get an electric car.

Reality: The planet should be polluted. Why? Because it is. That's reality.

The payoff for letting go of the belief: Clarity. Action without anger.

Go back to your belief and reverse it a few times. First, change "She," He," and "They" to "I" or "My Mind." Play with sentences until you come up with reversals that ring true.

You have learned Katie's two techniques for letting go of beliefs, judgments, projections, or false perceptions. First, you asked, "Can I really know that?" You got a "No" answer and were left with reality. Second, you reversed your belief and got out of another person's business. The reversal helped you know yourself better.

To explore beliefs further, contact The Work Foundation, Inc., which offers workshops all over the world, books, tapes, and a website (www.thework.org). For information, call (877) 584-3967, or email: thework@thework.org.

⤳

We don't see things as they are; we see things as we are.

—Anaïs Nin

DAY 13

Edit Your Projects

Task: *Today, examine all of the projects you have not completed. To locate them, look into files, inside drawers, in closets, and under the bed. As they surface, make a list of things you promised yourself, or others, to do. Divide the list into Big Projects and Small Projects.*

See how many you come up with in 30 minutes. Then ask yourself, "Which projects can be jettisoned? Which are a burden? Which ones are totally unrealistic? Which ones am I willing to start today?"

Finally, drop one project from your life and box up all of its paraphernalia. You know what we are talking about—paint sets, knitting needles, unread magazines, and plans for building a dome-shaped doghouse. Finally, place the supplies to be recycled in the trunk of your car.

Each project you have in your life complicates it. After you have completed the task above, you will see how overcommitted you are to *optional* jobs, hobbies, and activities. Even though many of your projects are small, like framing a picture, any unfinished project can bog you down.

We are talking about voluntary complexity.

If you have no special projects, you still have hundreds of commitments. On the home front, there's paperwork—bills to pay, insurance to buy, investments to manage, bank accounts to balance, credit cards to track, and family history to collect. Then there's housekeeping—vacuuming, dusting, dishwashing, laundry, and dry cleaning.

And what about meals? You plan, shop, prepare, cook, serve, and clean up after each one. Unfortunately, pizzas, frozen dinners, and delicatessen takeouts cannot be served nightly (though more and more Americans are doing just that).

What about landscape management? Trees, shrubs, and lawns must be watered, fertilized, pruned, weeded, mowed, and edged (unless you live in an apartment). Just when the yard is under control, you find yourself wondering: Do I need a new roof? When will the siding need to be repainted? Do I need a storm door? Does the deck need to be repaired? If you're a renter, you delegate these jobs to the landlord (who gets revenge by raising your rent).

What about kids and pets? The more you have, the more you work. At the very least, one child doubles the number of chores you perform. Animals require less care but must be fed, groomed, housed, and taken to the vet.

We have a lot to do, and much of it is self-imposed.

The Cookbook Project

It's so easy to become infatuated with new ideas. Five years ago, Cris became enamored with the idea of writing a vegetarian cookbook. With her interest in simplification, she envisioned a unique cookbook based on intuitive thinking and no measurements for ingredients. Within six months, she had acquired a mountain of cookbooks as well as hundreds of recipes from magazines. She was committed—and then inertia set in. Here is what she wrote in her journal about the experience:

"I had a dream to write a cookbook titled *Intuitive Cuisine*. But the reality was quite different—I was too busy doing other things. On Monday evening, I decided to drop the cookbook project. Over a period of two hours, I pondered each book and tossed all but one. A drawerful of recipes went into my wood-burning stove. In the future, I will be more realistic about how much time I have. I will become less enthralled with new ideas." Cris took her cookbooks to William James Bookseller, a used bookstore, and received two hundred dollars in credit toward new books.

Learn to Say "I Don't Think So"

Saying "No" is difficult. This is a great truth, one of the greatest. It's so much easier to be nice, to be polite, to say "Yes," when you don't really mean it, or "Sure, I'll do it," when you have other things you'd rather do.

We have a solution. Instead of saying "No," say "I don't think so," a gentler phrase that is firm yet incontestable. Can anyone claim that you do think so when you say you don't? We don't think so. What follows are three situations that demonstrate how the tactful phrase "I don't think so" can simplify your life:

- Your teenage daughter begs you to hem her dress two hours before a dance that she has known about for six months. You have a dinner date. You smile and say: "I don't think so."
- Your husband asks if he can bring his five buddies home for dinner after you have just taken the bar exam. Your response: "I don't think so."
- You are asked to be secretary for the baseball team because you are the only one who has a computer and you were the organizer last year. You say: "I don't think so."

"I don't think so" is never followed by an excuse or an apology. You need not say: "I don't think so—I'm so sorry." Or "I don't think so—I'm too tired." Follow the phrase with silence.

Three Little Words That Can Change Your Life

The most important advice presented in this chapter is contained in three little words—"Do It Now." When someone asks you to do something or you decide to take on a new project, ask yourself, "Can I do it now?" If you can, you will radically simplify your life. Why?

1. *You will handle some jobs once.* If you do it immediately, or as soon as possible, you won't have to commit it to memory or write it down on a Post-it, on your calendar, or in your date book. Scheduling takes time and energy— "Where can I fit it in?" Look forward to seeing a sparsely filled schedule.

2. *People will be amazed by your competence.* You will be regarded as a person who keeps his word, who can be trusted. You will receive kudos, flowers, and promotions.

3. *You will receive fewer penalties.* You will get fewer fines, phone calls, and late charges for forgetting to fulfill your obligations. Penalties are complicators.

4. *You may not have the ability to do it later.* No matter how much we plan, we can't know what lies ahead. Don't procrastinate.

5. *You will be done with it.* Your mental hard drive won't fill up with undone tasks. By the way, procrastinators suffer 20 percent more ailments than do nonprocrastinators, says psychologist Dianne Tice of Case Western University.

Project Simplifiers

We have only 24 hours in a day. What is the best way to match the number of commitments to the number of hours in a day?

Make a red check mark by tips that will simplify your commitments.

❑ **Rethink multitasking.**
Multitasking means "doing two or more tasks at once." Today

we are programmed to eat while we're watching television, cook while we're on the phone, pay bills while we ride the commuter train, and flip through papers as we listen to our answering machine. Most tasks deserve your undivided attention: Talking to your mate. Playing with your kids. Brushing your dog. Making a vegetable lasagna.

❏ Do one special project at a time.
If you put your heart and soul into one special project at a time, your life will become much simpler.

❏ Make a three-ring binder for magazine articles.
If you collect articles for projects, put them in a binder with dividers naming your favorite subjects—book reviews, gardening tips, and travel destinations. Take your notebook on car trips, plane flights, and to local cafés. When your notebook is filled, transfer the "keepers"—reference articles—to a permanent binder on each subject.

❏ For Serious Simplifiers only!
Collect *all* your unfinished and unstarted projects. Next, toss your projects and the paraphernalia that goes with them. Who knows what new interests you may discover if you free yourself of the deadweight of old business. Remember how good it felt when you finished final exams and could throw out your notes?

∽

Take your life in your own hands and what
happens? A terrible thing: no one to blame.

—Erica Jong

DAY 14

Combat Information Overload

Task: *Today, go around your house with a shopping bag and fill it with outdated magazines, catalogues, newsletters, newspapers, brochures, and books. Put the magazines and books in the trunk of your car to be taken to the library or your health club. Put the rest in your recycle bin. Finally, make a pile of newsletters and clipped magazine articles that you intend to read immediately.*

Information is everywhere. Our challenge is to control the constant stream of data that flows into our lives and to divert information that is not useful or uplifting.

Figure out the easiest way to become informed. Choose the best news source you can find. It might be a weekly newsmagazine, news on the Internet, a daily newspaper, or the Sunday *New York Times*. Or you could listen to radio or television news. Decide when you want to hear the news. Just because the news comes on at six o'clock, you don't have to watch it at six. You can tape it and watch it at your convenience. Remember, you can read, hear, or watch the news 24 hours a day—so be selective.

Each weekday morning, before school, video producer Jeannine Yeomans and her two daughters watch the *Today* show or *Good Morning America* while they eat breakfast. During the news, they discuss the issues as they come up. This is one way to become informed.

Cris says, "To be informed, I skim a newsmagazine. I try not to fall for fabricated stories like the one in the movie *Wag the Dog*. My challenge is not to become saddened by the fact that so many important stories—like the state of the Earth—are ignored or downplayed."

Connie says, "I like to be informed about world events. I am interested in how the news affects my life, my kids' lives, and our future. I'm interested in social trends." She reads the daily news on the internet, subscribes to the Sunday *New York Times* and the weekly newsletter, *Bottom Line*.

Attorney Tom Landis says, "I go through waves of reading the paper and not reading the paper. I don't read newspapers regularly because I find them uninformative, incomplete, and depressing. Too much news is oriented toward disasters. I find the information we need to function in society comes to us six or seven times a day."

Earl Warren, the Chief Justice of the United States Supreme Court, said. "I read the sports page first because it is a record of man's accomplishments—and the front page last because it's a record of his failures."

Audrey, an active member of her community, is adamant about the importance of reading local news. "I have to know what's going on in my community to be a responsible part of it. If I choose not to know, then I must deal with the consequences. Certainly, not everything in the newspaper is honest or complete. I don't read everything with the same depth. I read the headlines, the first sentences, and the articles that interest me."

Newspaper reporter Gil says, "There's a real difference between newspapers. Some papers really try to get information to people. They do thorough investigations and have few sacred cows—stories they won't tackle. Other papers shy away from covering the news. Most of their articles are PR and wire service stories. As a reporter, I try to give readers facts that will enable them to decide whether to become involved in an issue."

Know which type of newspaper you read.

If you watch the late night news right before you go to sleep, think about what it does to your dreams. Does it create visions of dancing wood nymphs or skulking fugitives? Dr. Andrew

Weil, author of *Spontaneous Healing*, says, "The news has a profound effect on people. I think it makes them anxious, angry, and outraged. And those are not useful emotions. They don't help your body."

Instead of overdosing on news, gossip, and information, write in a notebook for a week and let information come from within, reflecting your own thoughts and feelings.

Edit Your Magazines

If you are like most people, your home is filled with stacks of unread magazines, beautiful magazines with fascinating articles. Would your life be simpler if you stopped some of those subscriptions? Unread magazines can feel like homework. Homework that never ends.

When it comes to magazines, less is more.

- Instead of subscribing to magazines, occasionally buy one magazine and go to a café to read it.
- Get on an airplane or go to the beach with one wonderful magazine. Remove the cards, perfume ads, and thick paper inserts. It will feel better to handle.
- If you travel by car, take all of your unread magazines on a trip and return home with none.
- Read the latest magazines at your local library, where you can copy the best articles for future reading.
- When browsing through a magazine for the first time, tear out articles you want to read (rather than dog-earring pages). Staple the pages together. Connie keeps a small stack of articles beside her bed. She tosses them or passes them along after she reads them.

To control magazines:

- Recycle magazines weekly. On the day before recycling day, go around the house with a grocery bag and collect old magazines and catalogues.

- Designate a basket, bag, or shelf space for magazines that will go to others. Give them another life.
- If you are involved in a retail business or professional service, create a magazine trading basket/rack for the customers. Attach a sign that says, "Take me, I'm yours."
- If you use some magazines for research (like *Sunset, Architectural Digest, Communication Arts*), create a special place for these on a shelf. When a new one arrives, file the old ones immediately.
- Display current magazines face out. Stacked magazines are never seen. Putting them in baskets doesn't show them off either. Get them off the floor and your coffee table. Instead, create a wall rack or hang some clipboards.

Stop Stockpiling Books

Jerry Seinfeld said, "What's this obsession with books? Are they trophies? Why do we need them after we read them?" Most people's bookshelves are teeming with unread books.

What's happening? We buy books for a variety of reasons. We buy a book because it received rave reviews. Or we like the cover. Or the concept. Or it was a best-seller. *But once we put it down, we can't pick it up again.* We lose momentum. Inertia sets in. We become distracted by other activities or a newer book.

Recycle some of your unread books today. Let go of the guilt. Let go of paperbacks, hardbacks, almanacs, boxed sets, series, and deluxe editions. No books are off limits. If you decide later that you want to read a book you have tossed, you'll probably find it at a used bookstore or the local library.

Mia, Cris's sister, stopped stockpiling books. "I purchase one book at a time, read it, and then pass it on to a friend. I limit the number of books in my reference library to twelve." Her keepers include Daniel Quinn's *Ishmael* and Stephen Mitchell's *Tao Te Ching.* She rereads these books, gleaning new insights with each reading.

Obviously, a book collection is a personal matter. If you are a professional, your job may require that you maintain a personal reference library. As for your other books, pass them along as soon as you are done with them. Give them a short shelf life.

After you read it, why do you need it?

Info-Simplifiers

As we move through the nineties and into the next millennium, we are being faced with the challenge of having to sift through escalating amounts of information. To combat the deluge, look for new ways to screen out what you see, hear, and read.

Make a red check mark by tips that will simplify information.

❏ **Radically reduce your reading pile.**
To simplify, read *one* book or magazine at a time. Read it and be done with it. When you skim magazines full of ads and little substance, remove the interesting articles. Staple the pages together and place them in a flat rectangular basket for future reading. Look at the ads once.

❏ **Discourage information from phone solicitors.**
Create one-liners that don't invite comebacks: "You have the wrong number"—"I don't take phone solicitations"—"I'm the housesitter"—"She's teaching English in Japan."

❏ **Discover news on the Net.**
Major newspapers are on the Web. Internet news is free, fresh, and won't get ink on your fingers. You won't have to recycle papers or stop delivery when you go on vacation.

❏ **Beam up censored news on the Internet.**
Sonoma State University's website can inform you about news that isn't featured in the mainstream media. Read their top ten censored stories of the year at www.sonoma.edu. Click on "Special University Programs" and then on "Project Censored."

❏ **Take fewer notes.**
Do you take reams of notes, which you pile, file, and never read? Take fewer notes, and when you do take them, incorporate them into your life immediately. Floating notes clutter your desktop and your mind.

❏ **Pick up fewer brochures.**
Be selective when you reach out to take a brochure, wherever you are, and bring home *fewer* brochures when you visit fairs and expos. When you are tempted to pick up a business card sitting on a counter, think twice. You'll have to find a place for these papers when you get home, and no doubt will have to toss them in the future.

❏ **Read newsletters for quickie news.**
Cancel subscriptions to magazines and newspapers in favor of reading a comprehensive newsletter, such as *Bottom Line*.

❏ **Put doors on your bookshelves.**
Besides books, bookshelves often collect all kinds of clutter. Install doors on your bookshelves to make your office more serene.

❏ **Get rid of objects with messages on them.**
When you reach into your clothes closet, are you blasted with messages on T-shirts? When you reach for a mug, are you hit with witticisms? When you look at your refrigerator door, do magnets scream out "Beware of Snack Attacks" and "Look like Twiggy, not Miss Piggy"? Messages are distracting.

❏ **Display kids' books face out.**
Make a rack that displays the covers of children's books. A book rack, in addition to a bookshelf, sends kids the message that "Books are important." Once a week, put away the old books and feature several new ones. Kids are more apt to read books if they can see the covers—and when they look new and different.

❏ For Serious Simplifiers only!

Go on a "Low-Information Diet." Say "No!" to extraneous information for *one week*. Just read what you must for your profession. Don't read irrelevant articles in magazines, newspapers, and newsletters. Avoid catalogues and self-improvement books. Shun the television. In your car, don't listen to radio shows or mind-bending tapes. Instead, play soothing music from tapes or CDs. Finally, dodge advertising where possible. Consume fewer info-calories.

∽

> *To bypass information, go backpacking in a national park.*
>
> —Smokey the Bear

DAY 15

Design Simple Systems

Task: *Today seek, sort, and organize the keys to everything in your life—cars, boats, bike locks, gates, sheds, houses, and offices. Purchase key labelers and rings and make duplicates, if needed. Finally, create a place just for keys.*

Install a rack or board with pegs or nails and label it so missing keys can be identified. This system works well for duplicate and seldom-used keys.

For everyday keys, we have three suggestions: (1) Put a basket by the front door for family members to deposit their keys. (2) Hang a hook inside your entry door. (3) Provide each family member with his own complete set of keys.

Keys that are organized can make your life easier—but keys that aren't can drive you crazy.

We love organization. We have noticed that when our external environment is organized, our internal, emotional environment reflects it. Before we organize, we simplify as much as possible. Sometimes we simplify several times before we organize.

Simplify, then organize. Always in that order.

When you *simplify* an area of your home, you reduce the number of items in it. For example, when you simplified your closet on Day 5, you let go of seldom-worn clothing. *Organizing* is a very different process. To organize, assign each item a special place and a way of being in that place.

To make functioning in your storage areas simpler, fill them less than three-quarters full. Keeping space around items on shelves, in drawers, and in the fridge makes them easier to find and put away. In general, hanging things is more efficient than placing things in drawers, and drawers are more accessible than cupboards.

When organizing, watch out for roommates and family members who make work by dropping their stuff all over the house. Encourage them to put their possessions in designated areas. For example, you might earmark the coffee table for your mate's current reading material—and agree to put *your* books and magazines elsewhere.

Shake Up Your Random Systems

A *system* is basically a habit, the way you do a task repeatedly. The routines you use to grocery shop, do laundry, and clean your house are all systems. Any repeated steps that lead to the completion of a task form a system.

There are two kinds of systems: Random Complex Systems and Planned Simple Systems. There is an enormous difference between the two. A simple system requires forethought and planning. A complex system is the result of doing something thoughtlessly, haphazardly. Here are some examples of complex systems:

- Hem a Dress Before the Party system
- Pay the Bills After the Bill Collector Calls system
- Go on a Diet When Your Clothes Don't Fit system
- Tune Up Your Car When It Smokes system

The complex systems we just mentioned are *stressors*. They can make you feel angry, anxious, and unbalanced. By contrast, simple systems do not disturb your peace of mind. You feel grounded while operating them.

In a planned system, there is a place for everything and everything is kept in its place. For example, the perfect location for dishes would be the cupboard most convenient to where the dishes are dried.

To keep things in their place, planned systems utilize hooks, bins, boxes, trays, dividers, labels, and lazy Susans. Look for organizers in catalogues, variety stores, hardware stores, and specialty stores like Hold Everything and Stacks & Stacks.

Before you design a system, give it a name. Naming a system dignifies it. Instead of telling someone, "I'll show you how to do the laundry," we proudly say, "Let me show you The Laundry System." Other examples of systems: The House Cleaning System, The Grocery Shopping System, The Car Maintenance System, and The Pet Care System.

To keep your systems running smoothly, review them frequently. As new things come in, encourage old things to flow out. When things stop flowing out, we call it Systems Overload.

Other people can undermine your systems. To avoid Systems Sabotage, patiently show your housemates how to operate your systems. Tell them why you like your systems and why they simplify your life—and may simplify theirs, too!

Systematize Everything

What follows are some examples of Planned Simple Systems. You can devise a time-saving system for anything you do repeatedly.

Make a red check mark by the systems that will simplify your life.

❏ **The Recycling System**
Recycling is here to stay. Create a system that is easy to use. For instance, in the kitchen, create a garbage area with one large trash can for regular trash and two smaller cans for recyclables, one for mixed paper and one for cans and bottles. By the back door, keep a basket for newspapers. In your mail-handling area, keep a trash can and a mixed-paper recycling basket—for junk mail, catalogues, and computer paper.

Become more conscious of how much you recycle and make an effort to reduce that amount. By reducing the quantity, you will simplify your life and protect the environment—our nest! Cris's outdoor garbage can is less than half-filled each week. She buys most of her food in bulk and composts her peelings. When she stops for groceries, she carries a large African basket and several recycled plastic produce bags.

❏ The Forms System
Custom-made financial information forms can help you manage your life. Create a format, collect the data, and keep them current. Keep your forms in a binder in a safe place, away from curious eyes. Here are some examples:

- *The General Information Form:* Basic information about family members. Include each person's name, birthday, social security number, driver's license number, and passport number. Note expiration dates. Next, write: "Where is," followed by lines titled Passport, Birth Certificate, Marriage Certificate, and Armed Services papers, and record the place where you stored each item.
- *Professional Relationships:* Include the name, address, and phone number of your attorney, accountant, stockbroker, insurance broker, and investment advisor.
- *Bank Accounts:* Include the bank name, address, phone number, and account number of every personal or business bank account of each family member.
- *Safe Deposit Box:* Include the name of the bank, box number, location of the key, and a dated list of contents of the box.
- *Credit Cards:* Include the name, account number, expiration date, and phone number in case of loss for each credit card. Another solution is to photocopy all credit cards you normally carry with you.
- *Estate Plan:* List the name of your estate planning attorney, the location of your original will, and the names of trustees, executors, guardians, and the person who holds your durable power of attorney for medical or financial reasons.

- *Insurance:* List the broker, insurance company, policy numbers, and premium due date for your car, house, medical, and life insurance.

❏ The CDs and Tapes System

When Cris and Connie grew up, they had black plastic phonograph records in two sizes. In the nineties, the task of organizing entertainment is mind-boggling. Today, do yourself a favor and put the clutter of videos and tapes behind you.

Search the house for all your videotapes. Tuck them into their jackets, and find a place big enough to store them neatly. Put the rejects into a Recycle Pile.

Collect your CDs and the jewel boxes that protect them. Look everywhere. Make a Recycle Pile. Distribute the remaining CDs to their proper locations.

Find all your audio tapes hidden in cars, in drawers, and on shelves. Sort them into type—music, books on tape, self-help—and make a pile for the rejects. Put your favorites in a drawer or on a shelf. Finally, put the rejects from all three categories into your car to be given away.

Once you have listened to audio tapes, there is a good chance you will never listen to them again. Kate says, "I buy audio tapes for long drives from Sun Valley to San Francisco. After I listen to the tapes, I send them to the Gooding, Idaho, public library. Most of the people I know borrow tapes from libraries." Books on tape may also be rented from mail-order companies.

❏ The Ticket System

You receive flyers for the theater, lectures, and other events, and you discover events in the newspaper. Here is an easy three-step strategy for handling *ticketed* events.

1. Ask yourself, "Do I really want to go out or would I rather stay at home with my slippers on?" If you answer "Yes, I can't wait to go," write the event in your calendar.

2. Place the order form in your Bills to Pay Box/Stack, or write the phone number for ordering the tickets on your To Do list.

3. When your tickets arrive by mail, place them with the directions in a Pending Folder. You will always know where they are when it's time to go.

❏ Mini systems

These systems are less detailed than the previous systems, but demonstrate the importance of thinking things out.

- *The Eyeglasses System:* Collect your reading glasses, sunglasses, glasses cases, lens cleaners, and croakies. Find a place for these items. Put them in a box, drawer, or basket. You will always know where to find them.

- *The Shoes-by-the-Door System:* Shoes track in dirt, mud, small stones, and grass clippings. Floors are frequently damaged by shoes—high heels dent floors, black soles mar them, and grit from sneaker soles makes scratches. To remedy this situation, ask the members of your family to remove their shoes and leave them by the door as they enter the house. Your reward is less sweeping, less vacuuming, less carpet shampooing, and a quieter home.

- *The Picture Hanging System:* Take the agony out of hanging things. In a tackle box, put several sizes of picture hooks, small nails, some picture hanging wire, a hammer, masking tape and Post-its for marking, a pencil, and a measuring tape. Keep these tools together for hanging pictures.

- *The House Map System:* Design a printed map that tells people how to find your house. Print it in two sizes—an 8 ½ by 11–inch map for faxing and mailing, and a smaller size for your wallet, datebook, and invitations. The smaller size may be made by reducing the larger size on a copy machine.

❏ Systems for kids

Make raising kids simpler by systematizing some of their activities. Here are two examples. There are many more.

- *The Toy Library System:* Most kids are overwhelmed by the number of toys they have. Help your child live with less, and enjoy his toys more, by creating a secondary storage place/cupboard in another room or in the garage. Call it The Toy Library. Children can check out and return toys, as they do library books. Forgotten toys will seem like new ones.
- *The School Paper and Artwork System:* Find a basket or container for each child's school papers. Once a month or so, encourage your child to choose his favorites. If his artwork is bulky or hard to store, snap a photo of your child with the artwork. Create long-term storage for the keepers. Another idea: Put a piece of artwork in a large plastic box frame, hang it—and then encourage your child to change it frequently.

❏ Systems to consider

- *The Housecleaning System:* Designate one day a week for tackling house cleaning, then forget about it the rest of the week. For a simple system, read Jeff Campbell's *Speed Cleaning*.
- *The Laundry System:* Create a system with large white stackable wire baskets for clothing categories. Confine washing days to two days a week rather than doing it continuously.
- *The Grocery Shopping System:* Figure out the best days and times to grocery shop for the week. A preprinted grocery list simplifies this task.
- Refer to our book *Simply Organized!* (Perigee), for descriptions of systems in greater detail.

❏ **For Serious Simplifiers only!**

Systematize *everything* you do repeatedly. To find out what needs revamping, look for things you do randomly. Before you design a system, ask yourself, "Can I eliminate this routine completely?" Dropping a routine is the simplest system of all.

∽

> "*In order to seek one's own direction, one must simplify the mechanics of ordinary, everyday life.*"
>
> —Plato

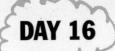

DAY 16

Set Up an Efficient Office

Task: *Today, declutter your desktop and surrounding counters. Spend at least an hour sorting and tossing. Make your work space the most efficient area in your life. Clutter is especially annoying when it is on your desk or in your office.*

Get control of your desktop today. Here's the way to do it: (1) Don't allow irrelevant objects on your desk—plants, trophies, souvenirs, and framed pictures. Okay, maybe one! (2) Always clean off your desk before you start a new project. (3) Before you leave your desk for the day, clear it off so you can start fresh the next day.

To simplify your complicated life, you will need a well-organized office whether it's in a converted closet, in an extra bedroom, or in a corner of the kitchen. To create a productive office, take an inventory of your tasks and equipment, then organize your surfaces and storage areas to suit your style of working.

Create your own version of a simplified office.

You should be able to perform multiple tasks in your office. Include the equipment you need to complete projects from start to finish. Furnish your office with good lighting (consider full-spectrum bulbs) and ventilation. To make your space more user-friendly, include artwork and photos on the walls. We love our offices. We can't imagine living without them.

Cris's Downtown Office

Cris arrives at her downtown office around 10:00 each morning, after an aerobics class. "I like to get exercise out of the way early," she says. After that, she spends the rest of the day in and out of her office.

In her 12 × 15–foot office, Cris has a Danish modern desk, computer, printer, scanner, bookcase, and an ergonomic chair. On the walls are two travel posters mounted on foam core, two bulletin boards, and an oil painting of oak trees. About her office she says, "I can't imagine organizing my life without a well-equipped office. I do so many things there. I make phone calls, handle correspondence, plan workshops, and write books. My office simplifies my life."

Connie's Home Office

"The most important thing about my office is—it's mine, all mine," says Connie. "Soon after my son was born, I created my first office—a desk in a corner of our den. That desk was off-limits to other family members. A few years later, my husband, Jon, and I set up a joint office where I had my own desk and my own computer.

"Currently, I have an office in my home overlooking our back garden. I spend an average of six hours a day in my office, so I make working there as much fun, stimulating, and convenient as possible. On my four by eight–foot bulletin boards, there are greeting cards, inspirational sayings, and dozens of photos of family and friends.

"I come into my office to get centered, to manage family and personal business, to do creative projects, and to run Home Management Systems, my consulting and speaking business. I have a computer, a laser printer, a color printer, a scanner, a copy machine, a plain paper fax machine, a postage scale, a Pitney Bowes postage meter, bookshelves, files, and a counter-height worktable. I try to keep all of the surfaces in my office clear so that I can work easily.

"Working at home is a simplifier. But there are drawbacks—it is hard to stay away from household maintenance and refrain from overworking. I find it hard to separate the business of running a home from the business of running a business, but the joy of having a flexible schedule and an integrated life makes up for it."

Conquer Mountains of Mail

Your mail and your key collection are barometers of the complexity of your life. We talked to several people who have definite "steps" for opening mail. Then we combined our ideas with theirs to come up with this system:

Step 1: Toss out junk mail. When you sort your mail, sit next to a Mixed Paper Recycling Bin where you can toss your unsolicited junk mail and catalogues (cancel the ones you never want to see again).

Step 2: Separate catalogs, magazines, and weekly newspapers. Put your magazines and newspapers where family members are most likely to find them and read them. Create a basket for catalogs. Toss the old ones as you add new ones.

Step 3: Open the important mail. Open the envelopes of the important mail—with an easy-to-use letter opener—and toss the outer envelopes and junky inserts.

Step 4: Separate your mail into categories.

- Bills to Pay: If you pay your bills once or twice a month, you can leave them unopened in a bill file.
- Charitable Requests: File them for future consideration.
- Drop-Dead Mail: Crucial matters that need attention.
- Possibilities: Things to read and do—if you have the time.
- Filing: Things to keep that don't require action.

Don't Pile It—File It!

With a simple, reasonable, thoughtful, and usable filing system—not the national archives—it is fast, easy, and painless to file the papers you must keep. Create useful and broad categories for your filing system. Here are some suggestions for topics and subtopics.

ACTIVE FILES (Clear out these files at the end of each calendar year.)
Household
Monthly Bills & Receipts
Home Maintenance & Remodeling (Keep until you sell your house.)
Travel (Include frequent flyer mileage information.)
Projects (family, educational, or volunteer)
Children & Family
Investments & Banking (Keep three years for income tax purposes.)
Business

IMPORTANT DOCUMENTS FILES (Keep these files available as long as you own the items they represent.)
Home Title & Mortgage Papers
Car Title & Registration Papers
Investments
Real Estate Title Documents
Stock Purchase Confirmations

INACTIVE FILES (Separate these files from your active files.)
Financial Files (Keep these files according to IRS guidelines)
Personal Files
Children's Files (Keep children's mementos or records in a box from September 1 to August 31 and then file them.)

Make Active Files into Inactive Files Yearly.

- At the end of the calendar year, clean out your files and transfer them to your inactive files in a banker's box or filing cabinet.
- Then set up your new files for the upcoming year.

Create and dismantle your new files frequently.

- When you have a piece of paper with no designated file folder, create a new file instead of piling stray papers on your desk. Later, eliminate the file or merge it with another one.
- When you have a piece of paper, or a stack of papers, that represents a project, make a file and place the activity on your To Do list. Then put the file away to keep from having small files all over your office.

To keep your filing cabinets from becoming crammed full, know what to toss and what to keep.

- *Toss* duplicates, outdated material, and things you want but don't need.
- *Toss* articles you don't have time to read and data you seldom refer to.
- *Toss* material you can easily find elsewhere.
- *Save* it if it's the only copy and replication would be difficult. Or if you will need to refer to the information again soon. Or if you are required by law to keep it. Or if it is an integral part of a client or project file.

Office Simplifiers

We encourage you to try any idea that might make your office more efficient. What follows are things we have tried and liked.

Place a check mark in the boxes by the tips that will simplify your office.

❏ **Give the gift of a handwritten note.**
We enjoy giving and receiving handwritten notes. When you create a simple system for correspondence, dashing off a note takes a minute.

- Place pretty note cards, envelopes, stamps, and a favorite pen in a basket on your desk or in a drawer in another room of the house.
- Make personalized notecards. Take your picture in front of a white wall and copy it in black and white onto card stock. Fold it, write on the inside, and tape the card shut.

❏ Create a Pending Folder.

This folder holds theater tickets, invitations, and directions to events. When you are ready to leave for an event, know where to find information. This folder can also contain gift certificates and store credits. Check it often and keep it current. Using a Pending Folder is less cumbersome than carrying around tickets and information in your purse or date book.

❏ Create an Upcoming Trips Folder.

When you book a trip, file your itinerary, airline tickets, hotel confirmations, and general information about the trip in an Upcoming Trips Folder. Take this folder with you on your next trip.

❏ If you collect names of restaurants and places to go . . .

When you read an article about a new restaurant or place to visit, don't file it—add the name, location, phone number, and a sentence about the place to a datebook page dedicated to Restaurants to Try or Places to Visit. Or keep a running list on your computer. *Free yourself from the weight of files filled with possibilities.* You can always get information from a library, bookstore, the Internet, travel agency, or by making a phone call.

❏ Create a supplies drawer.

To be highly organized and to run fewer errands, keep this drawer well stocked. Keep extra tape, batteries, pencils, pads, inkjet cartridges, labeling tape, Rolodex cards, Post-it notes, and checks in a supply drawer (or cupboard).

❏ Make binders with clear sheet protectors.

Use binders with clear cover holders for organizing all sorts of things—recipes, gardening information, ideas for vacations, and creative ideas from magazines. Label the spines and slip artwork, postcards, or an 8 × 10–inch color-copied photo into the cover. Keep several in stock. These binders are inexpensive and easy to label.

❏ **Make a warranties binder.**
Place your warranties, instruction manuals, and receipts of purchase in clear sheet protectors in a binder. Put a labeled sticker on the front of each sheet protector to quickly identify each product. Make an index page.

❏ **Keep manuals for office machines handy.**
Keep manuals and instructions for your fax, copier, and phone answering machine under the machines they represent. A real time saver!

❏ **Simplify your life with a Rolodex.**

- *Keep your Rolodex up to date*. Each time you receive a number from phone information or elsewhere—for a new client, friend, or business—make a new Rolodex card. Eliminate scraps of paper with numbers. When someone's address or phone number changes, update your Rolodex immediately.
- *Use your Rolodex cards for other information*. Put directions on the back and take the card when you go somewhere for the first time. You can also use Rolodex cards to record birthdays and names of children.
- *Use Rolodex cards as your personal Yellow Pages*. Keep track of names of vendors or service people by making Rolodex cards with categories, such as Plumber and Dog groomer. When you are given the name of a person with a service, you can find them without knowing their name.

❏ **Keep your address book on the computer.**
Putting your addresses onto the computer takes time but will save you time in the long run.

- Computer address labels are useful for many things—business flyers, baby announcements, and Christmas cards.
- Address lists can be printed in various sizes and used as phone/address books. Carry copies in your car, briefcase, or Daytimer. Place a copy by phones.
- Place incoming envelopes with address changes beside your computer and make the changes the next time you use your computer.

❏ Make an index of your files.
Make an index of your files so you can quickly figure out whether passports are filed under "P" for Passports or "T" for "Travel."

❏ Use an answering machine.
Make calls during off-hours and receive detailed responses while you are away. Make sure your answering system can handle long messages. Get a digital answering machine, an answering machine with a long tape, or voice mail from the phone company.

❏ Make pads with used printer paper.
Use the backside of used printer paper for faxing and rough drafts. Connie has her recycled paper cut and padded with a piece of cardboard on the back. Cuts cost one dollar; padding is two dollars. Pads of paper won't get confused with loose important papers.

❏ Use a scrapbook to clear off your desk and bulletin board.
When you have something on your desk or bulletin board that you can't bear to toss because it brings up a happy memory, paste it into a scrapbook or toss it into a memory box. Use this method at least twice a week.

❏ Connie's can't-do-without favorite office tools.
Think about adding tools that will improve your office life.

- *Label machine.* Create wonderful plastic labels for boxes, binders, files, folders, and kids' possessions.

- *Postage scale.* Spend less time waiting in lines at the post office. Electronic scales, which sell for less than $75, show the weight of a letter or package as well as the first, third, and international air postage costs.
- *Business card punch.* This handy gadget makes business cards into Rolodex cards, so you do not have to cut cards down and staple them onto Rolodex cards.
- *Stamp for depositing checks.* Instead of writing "For Deposit Only" and your signature on the back of your checks, have a stamp made with your deposit information. Run your home like a business.
- *Hole punches.* The 3-hole punch enables you to organize your papers into a notebook or binder format. The 1-hole punch has many uses. Connie uses it for attaching gift cards to gifts and small pieces of paper into her date book.
- *Laminating paper.* (It works like contact paper.) Connie often laminates something, such as a label, punches a hole in it, and runs a string through it. A great way to make luggage tags.
- *Permanent marking pens.* In the office, use permanent markers to address packages. In the kitchen, use them to label dishes to be taken to parties. In the laundry room, use it to personalize clothing.
- *One-step dividers for notebooks/binders.* Dividers come in sets of five, eight, ten, and thirty-one. No more labeling tabs. The first page is an index—make copies of it so you can change it.
- *Low-stick removable Scotch tape.* Connie uses it daily to attach things she doesn't want to ruin with regular tape. She tapes notes to her date book, papers onto painted surfaces, and decorations onto gifts.
- *Removable poster tape.* Connie thinks this tape is 3M's greatest invention. This tape affixes things like cards and photos to painted surfaces without damaging the paint. Give a roll to your kids for their posters.
- *CD opener.* Not a necessity, but Connie loves it. "Every time I open the shrink wrap around a CD, I'm glad I own this tiny tool. It comes with Velcro, so I attach it to the side

of my computer. Music buffs can attach it to the side of their CD player."

❏ **For Serious Simplifiers only!**
Spend several hours ruthlessly editing your files. If you don't have a filing cabinet, buy an inexpensive filing box to organize your important papers.

∽

Simplicity means having updated files.

DAY 17

Organize Your Computer Life

Task: *To simplify your computer life, make three piles: pile one, manuals; pile two, floppy discs and CD-ROMs; and pile three, registration materials and bills of sales. Read on to discover how to handle these piles.*

What is it about today that is so different from twenty years ago, when it was less difficult to find time to whip up an angel food cake, organize a family picnic, or insert pictures into a photo album? What has occurred to make *time* our most valued commodity? The answer is—technology.

When we were growing up, technology meant one telephone, a typewriter, a washing machine, and a black-and-white television. Today, it means a house full of machines that must be mastered, maintained, and programmed.

Computers, modems, and e-mail were supposed to make our lives simpler, and in some respects these technologies have, but they have also brought a host of new challenges. For instance, we must find *space* for the computer and its paraphernalia. We must develop new *organizational skills* to manage the influx of information. And, most of all, we must create *time* to use all of these technologies effectively.

Organize Your Computer Manuals

After you have done the sorting task at the top of the page, focus on the pile of manuals. There are three types of manuals to organize.

Handle your hardware manuals

Hardware manuals come with your computer, printer, modem, Zip drive, scanner, and digital camera. They explain how your hardware and peripherals work. If you have upgraded your computer equipment, such as your modem or printer, make sure you know which manual goes with which machine. To avoid confusion, record the date of purchase and the serial number of your equipment on the cover of the manual. It is a big pain to look behind or under the computer when you need to know the serial number. Also, write the technical support phone numbers inside the manual.

Keep track of your software program manuals

Software makes your computer perform different tasks such as word processing, spreadsheets, and games. In this group are programs such as Microsoft Word, Lotus 1-2-3, Pagemaker, Photoshop, and games like Myst. These manuals are essential for learning how to install programs and use them to their best advantage. It is common to upgrade programs by buying the latest version. When your new software arrives, clearly write the date of receipt and serial number on the manual. It helps to write the name of the program and its version on the spine of its manual—you will not always find it there. To avoid confusion, put your old disks and manuals in another location (or recycle them). Keep the new away from the old.

Deal with your utilities manuals

Utilities make your computer run more smoothly, make it more fun, or protect it in some way. Utilities include such programs as screen savers, virus protectors, and font jugglers. Utilities can be confusing. Keep these manuals together the way you did with your software program manuals.

Remove the outdated manuals

Put your current manuals back on the shelf. Put the program manuals, which you use frequently, closest to you, and the system manuals, which are used less often, farthest away.

Organize Your Disks and CD-ROMs

Sort your computer disks by program.

- If you have several versions of one software program, group them by version. For example, ClarisWorks version 1, 2, 3, and 4. With a rubberband, bind the floppies that compose a program.
- On the first disk or on the CD-ROM, mark the version number and serial number of the program. (When you call for technical support, you will be asked for your serial number to verify that you are the legal owner.)
- Put the date you acquired the latest version on the first disk. If you can't remember, put today's date. At least you know today that this version is the latest.
- Get rid of old versions of programs. Either store them, since you may need them for an old computer with an old operating system, or erase the disks and use them as blanks. Label them "BLANK," so you won't mistake them for important programs.

Review your CD-ROMs
It is easy to acquire useless CD-ROMs—they come in the mail and are given away. Some may be samples of programs you will never use. Pull out the important ones and toss the rejects.

Store your disks and CD-ROMs in these categories:

- System/peripherals
- Programs
- Games
- Communication software (America Online, fax/modem)
- Fonts
- Graphics
- Back-up disks
- Blank disks

Handle Your Receipts and Registrations

Step 1: Register your products.

Register your software and hardware as soon as possible after you purchase it. As a registered owner, you become eligible for technical support, inexpensive upgrades, and information about your product.

Step 2: Make a file for receipts and registrations.

Organize your receipts and copies of registrations by type or date. Create a file called Receipts & Registrations. Keep the file handy for returns, repairs, and technical support. Make a list of phone numbers for customer support and technical help for this file.

Computer Simplifiers

Owning computer paraphernalia has become a complicated experience, a veritable nightmare, in a relatively short period of time.

Make a red check mark by the tips that will simplify your computer life.

❏ **Hide techno-clutter.**
If you don't like looking at the computer dripping with cords, hide it in an attractive cabinet with doors or build it into a closet.

❏ **Label all cords.**
Label cords with the name of the equipment they connect to. Write directly on the cords or on the plugs with a fine indelible felt-tip pen. Labeled cords greatly simplify the moving and setting up of equipment. Place your idle cords in zip-lock bags.

❏ **Make a list of technical support numbers.**
On your computer, create a database for the technical support

phone numbers of your software and hardware. (Be sure to make a hard-copy backup.) Or record the numbers in your address book. Or list them on a Rolodex card. Find computer support quickly—when you need it!

❏ For Serious Simplifiers only!
Keep your computer free of superfluous stuff. Delete programs you rarely use. Don't get lulled into buying new fonts, games, graphics, and utilities that you won't use. Frivolous programs slow down computers and create *clutter*—more CDs, more manuals, and more information to manage.

∽

Store less on your mental hard drive.

DAY 18

Go for Financial Freedom

Task: *To achieve financial freedom, first figure out what you have and then manage it well. Today, collect your documents that are associated with large assets— documents for your car, house, investments, and so on—and put them in one filing cabinet called Assets. For your house: file your deed, purchase contract, closing papers, title policy, and insurance papers. For investments: file confirmations, year-end statements, and tax reporting forms. For cars: file ownership papers, registration documents, and insurance papers.*

Once you have organized your assets and know what you have, you are in a position to ask, "What would financial freedom mean to me?" For many people it means having the resources to pursue the career and lifestyle of their choice. It means getting up in the morning and saying, "What would I like to do today?" not "What do I have to do?"

Financial freedom doesn't mean quitting a job you love. It means quitting a job you don't love and finding another. It means being able to take a year off—to become physically fit, to explore the Himalayas, to write the Great American Novel. Why don't more of us experience financial freedom?

In the *Simple Living* newsletter, publisher Janet Luhrs says, "We regularly and continually give our money away to other people so they can become wealthy, while we live paycheck to paycheck. We buy the latest cars, bigger houses (than we can afford), full wardrobes, daily lattes, and gadgets of all kinds. As a result, we are on treadmills, never allowing ourselves to create the lifestyle we want."

What follows are five steps to financial freedom. If you are already economically independent, skip down to the next section.

Step 1: Focus on freedom

Financial freedom doesn't happen accidentally. You must make it a goal, an objective, your biggest challenge. Then slice your biggest challenge into bite-sized pieces and tackle one piece at a time. For your first piece, read *Your Money or Your Life—Transforming Your Relationship with Money and Achieving Financial Independence* by Joe Dominguez and Vicki Robin (Penguin Books, $11.95).

Vicki Robin says, "The food we eat, the dwellings we live in, the clothing we wear, and how we entertain ourselves are coveted and imitated as the good life by people all around the world. The fact that thousands of us are now choosing to build up savings and simplify our lives could actually slow down the spread of consumerism."

Step 2: Shift to thrift

Here are some commonsense ways to put the brakes on spending:

- *Use one credit card.* A credit card is a convenience, not a money tree. Pay your card off monthly and avoid interest.
- *Cancel overdraft protection for your checking account.* Don't make it easy to write checks for money you haven't got.
- *Don't buy anything (but a home) on time.* Pay hard cash for cars, furniture, and home appliances. Check the classifieds for good deals on used goods.
- *Live in a smaller home than you can afford.* Pay off your home as soon as possible by making larger payments than your mortgage requires.
- *Avoid shopping.* Don't go to the mall or read catalogues

unless you absolutely need something. Keep tabs on how much you pay for food, shelter, health, clothing, transportation, and entertainment.

- *Spend less on going to work.* Calculate how much it costs to go to work. Include transportation expenses (bus/train tickets, bridge tolls, parking, gasoline, insurance premiums, wear-and-tear on your car), clothing costs (special clothes for work, dry cleaning, alterations), and the cost of lunches. Most of these costs are unavoidable. Save where you can. Buy clothing that lasts, take sack lunches, and use public transportation where possible. Be creative!

- *When you get a raise, don't raise your standard of living.* Save even more. Or pay off your car and home mortgage.

Step 3: Set up an automatic savings plan

Save a percentage of your monthly income. Instruct your bank to transfer money from your checking account to your savings account or retirement account. *Next, set aside money for an emergency.* Save two to three months' salary if you feel secure in your job. Set aside at least six months' salary if your job is shaky. Put it into an interest-bearing account at a bank or brokerage house.

Step 4: Max out your tax-deferred retirement plan

After you have put aside money for a rainy day, contribute the maximum amount allowed each year to your 401(k), IRA, or Keogh.

Step 5: Become a smart investor

To make your money grow, talk to experts and read books, articles, and newsletters on money management. "Leaving money in the bank is like putting a wool sweater in a hot dryer. If we let it sit too long, it will shrink before our eyes," says financial advisor Barbara Stanny. "Make your money grow faster than taxes and inflation can take it."

Men, Women, and Money

Connie was inspired to start her business, Home Management Systems, because, as an attorney, she dealt with people who were frustrated by the probate process. Her job was to help people sort through a mountain of paperwork after their spouse or parents died. She met people who didn't know where their automobile title documents were, the status of their life insurance or medical insurance, where their stock certificates were, or who the executor of the will was.

"Those poor souls had to pay attorneys, paralegals, and accountants to help them untangle their finances," says Connie. "Oddly, most of those people were competent in other areas of their lives."

Connie advises people to get their arms around their finances before a catastrophe happens. She urges them to become familiar with their files of official-looking papers. "Know what's going on," she says. "In a marriage, both spouses need to be fully informed in the event of a divorce, death, or disability."

What follows are some excellent books for women:

- *Prince Charming Isn't Coming—How Women Get Smart about Money* by Barbara Stanny, the daughter of one of the founders of H & R Block. Barbara grew up relying on her father, then her husband, to manage her money. But a devastating financial crisis became a dramatic wake-up call. She knew she had to take charge. But how? Her journey to financial enlightenment is inspiring.
- If your husband is managing the money, read *What Every Woman Should Know about Her Husband's Money* by Shelby White.
- Use Karen McCall's *Financial Recovery Workbook System*, a set of tools that addresses compulsive spending, underearning, and other self-defeating money behaviors. For information write 40 Sir Francisco Drake Blvd., San Anselmo, CA 94960.

Raising Kids Costs More Than a Ferrari

Children bring a lot of laughter and love to life. They also bring worry, fatigue, and expense. When you think about having children, consider the cost in blood, sweat, tears, and *dollars*.

Having children is no longer a financial benefit. We do not need them to work on the farm. Today, becoming a parent is optional. To learn about life without children, subscribe to the newsletter *Child Free Lifestyle*, 6966 Sunrise Boulevard, Suite 111, Citrus Heights, CA 95610.

Financial Simplifiers

For fifteen years, Cris worked as a dental hygienist, a noble dead-end job that supported her comfortably. Then one day she wondered—"What is a day of life worth? If a day of life is worth $600 and I earn $200, I lose $400 when I work." Shortly thereafter, she quit her profession and followed her bliss—writing and giving workshops. Since 1981, Cris has had six books published.

Make a red check mark by tips that will simplify your financial life.

❑ **Subscribe to simple living newsletters.**

- *Simple Living* is a quarterly newsletter with practical tips on how to live frugally in style. Fascinating true life stories are featured. For a sample copy, write to 2319 N. 45th Street, Box 149, Seattle, WA 98103; (206) 464-4800.
- *A Real Life* is a witty and informative newsletter published by Barbara McNally. "I wanted to make a newsletter that is quiet and reassuring, not scary. And I wanted to prove that if you eat whole foods and live frugally, you don't have to live in a VW bus." To receive 6 issues a year, send $30 dollars to 245 Eighth Avenue, Box 400, New York, NY 10011.

❏ Simplify bill paying.

Bills are a recurring intrusion. To make this process easier, try different strategies until you find what works best.

- *Pay bills the moment they arrive.* Open your bills with everything you need nearby—a checkbook, stamps, envelopes, a calculator, and a trash can.
- *Pay your bills twice a month.* Pay your bills on the 1st and 15th of each month. Keep them unopened in a folder until it is time to pay them.
- *Pay bills automatically.* Many bills can be paid automatically, either by credit card, computer, or by your bank's automatic withdrawal service. Good candidates for automatic payments are your utilities, telephone, Internet service, health club, and medical insurance.

❏ Get ready for taxes in January.

For many people, tax time is chaos. *It need not be.* At the beginning of the year, set up file folders for receipts, stock confirmations, donation acknowledgments, business expenses, and any other items required by the IRS.

❏ Hire a part-time bookkeeper.

To simplify bill paying and record keeping, hire a bookkeeper or administrative assistant for a few hours a month. Hiring such a person is becoming more and more popular because of the increased volume of financial paperwork and the increased complexity of filing taxes. The going rate for a person who can do basic data entry, simple financial tasks, and paper handling is approximately $15 per hour in the San Francisco Bay Area.

❏ Shorten your signature on your checks.

Connie changed her signature at the bank and for her credit cards. She changed it from Constance C. Cox to CCCox, which makes signing checks and credit card slips much faster. Cris shortened her signature, too.

❏ **Create a home for charge card receipts.**

Create an envelope or box for each charge card. (Hopefully, you have just one card.) Throughout the month, put your current receipts in the envelope. When you pay the bill, match the receipts with the bill. Toss the receipts that are not needed for returning items or tax purposes. Staple the rest to the bill and file.

❏ **Carry fewer cards.**

Instead of carrying a stack of cards, make a wallet-sized card for recording your important numbers. Include your social security number, health insurance number, phone credit card number, frequent flyer number, club membership numbers, and store credit card numbers. Make a photocopy of the card and file it. Just carry one credit card, your ATM card, your driver's license, and any cards you must have with you such as a security card for work or a card that needs to be "swiped" through the machine for detection.

❏ **For Serious Simplifiers only!**

Don't use your credit card for three months. Be resolute. Or, every time you use your credit card, deduct the amount in your checkbook. Better yet, trade in your credit card for a debit card. It automatically withdraws the amount from the bank. You'll spend less.

∽

There is only one success—to be able to spend your life in your own way.

—Christopher Morley

DAY 19

Run Fewer Errands

Task: *Today, create a box for errands. You can use a great-looking basket, plastic tub, or shopping bag. Whatever works. Keep it by the door and fill it with film to be developed, shoes to be repaired, purchases to be returned, and papers to be taken to the copy center. On errand day, take the box in the car. When you come home, it will be empty. What a feeling!*

Running errands can run you ragged. With 24-hour grocery stores and 24-hour copy centers, it's possible to run errands all day and all night.

Many people work all week and then use evenings, Saturdays, and Sundays to do errands and personal tasks. What happened to the Sabbath, the day of rest, when stores were closed and we spent time visiting friends?

Errands multiplied when we got automobiles. Our grandparents, traveling by horse and buggy, made weekly or monthly trips to town. Can we be more like them?

The serfs in the Middle Ages had more free time than we have today. At the beginning of the Renaissance, religious holidays in some parts of Europe guaranteed people more than 150 days of revelry each year. Now we have little time to do anything besides work. Why?

Collectively, our self-worth is tied not to how fully we experience life, but to how much we do. In her book *Gift from the*

Sea Anne Morrow Lindbergh wrote, "Too many activities and people and things. Too many worthy activities, valuable things and interesting people. It is not merely the trivial which clutters our lives, but the important as well."

If you want to make God laugh, show him your Filofax.

But what's the alternative? Well, for starters, you can ignore or weed out unnecessary errands. You can organize how you manage errands. And last, you can delegate some of the most tedious errands. What follows are descriptions of two types of errand runners:

1. The Unaware Errand Runner

She's a dreamer who runs errands in a trancelike state—and she always has errands to run. To her, errands are important work and crucial to her identity. Perhaps she believes, "I run errands, therefore I am."

The UER has trouble distinguishing between errands that are urgent and those that may be postponed. She uses errands to procrastinate. Instead of focusing on her top priorities, she spends an afternoon running irrelevant errands. Sometimes she uses errands to avoid being still.

2. The Aware Errand Runner

In sharp contrast to the woman above, the Aware Errand Runner has a plan of action, a scheme for doing errands, She has an Errand Day, one day a week devoted to errands. She has an Errand Basket, like the one we described in today's task, and she uses an Errand Circle: She plans her errands so she can drive to them without backtracking. Then at the end of the day, she clears out the inside of her car so she will be ready for her next errand day—hopefully, a week later!!

Whenever the AER buys an item, she thinks about the number of errands it will require over its lifetime. "Will it break down?" "Will it need to be refilled frequently?" "Will it need to be professionally cleaned?"

This woman values her time. She keeps errand running in perspective. She runs errands—they don't run her!

Should You Hire an Errand Runner?

Everything you delegate frees up time to do something more pleasurable or more important. In her seminars, Connie says, "Delegating extends the results of what one person can do to what one person can manage. It lightens your workload by assigning others tasks you normally would do, but don't have the time or inclination to do."

"But only wealthy people can afford to delegate." Not really. You can hire low-salaried people, such as college students, high school students (they love to drive), seniors, and people who can use extra money. Provide (what you consider) bad jobs to good people.

"But if I delegate, the job won't get done right." Naturally, there are errands that require your expertise or presence, but many can be done by others. If you are worried about the job being done effectively, be open to the possibility that your hireling may know a faster, better, more cost-effective way. Everyone perceives the world differently.

Deciding whether to delegate errands is a tough one. Many people are comfortable hiring a cleaning person, a gardener, and a baby-sitter—but an Errand Runner? Be open to this concept.

Errand Runners can save you an incredible amount of time. They can deliver and pick up film, library books, dry cleaning, and items to be repaired—shoes, appliances, and the vacuum. They can take the pets to the vet or groomer. They can take the car to be serviced, washed, and fueled. They can pick up hats for the baseball team and vitamins from the health food store. They can return purchases, go to the post office, pick up office supplies, drugstore supplies, and household products, and, best of all, do the grocery shopping or pick up take-out food. In addition to running errands, they can do tasks around the house such as paying bills, doing laundry, wrapping presents, and contacting repair people.

But how do you know if you can use a runner effectively? Keep track of your chores and errands for a period of time, and then analyze them by type and regularity. Beside each, note the time needed to accomplish it. For example, notice how much time it takes to pick up one small item at a hardware store. If you have dozens of little things to do and shopping isn't your favorite pastime, consider hiring help.

To set up an Errand Runner, do these three things:

1. *Keep a running Errand List*. This list should be kept on a counter or in a drawer where you and the runner can easily find it. Keep it in a notebook with pockets for receipts, prescriptions, claim checks, return slips, and other papers needed for errands.
2. *Create an Errand Basket*. Include everything the runner needs for her errands—shoes to be repaired, videos to be returned, packages to mail. A Post-It note on each item can explain how to handle it.
3. *Create a simple way to pay*. Get a credit card, with a limit, just for her to use. Or create a cash drawer where receipts and accounting can be kept up to date by her. Or create a checking account with her signature, which she monitors and reports on to you.

Our friend Jeannine calls her Errand Runner a "Production Assistant," because she helps her produce a better quality of life for herself and her two daughters. Jeannine works full-time in a video production business and needs someone to do errands so she can spend her off-time with the kids. She says, "I am not willing to work well over 40 hours a week and then spend nights and weekends doing chores and errands that others can do as well or better." Jeannine pays her assistant $15 an hour.

Who Else Can Help You?

- *Hire a house cleaner*. Use this person creatively, to do jobs other than cleaning—lining drawers, sewing on buttons, and organizing your shelves. Schedule a repair person to come the day the cleaner is there and leave written instructions.

- *Hire a handyman (or woman) for your Honey-Do list.* Whether you have a husband or not, hire a handyman once a month (or two) to do things on your fix-it list. Delegate jobs like fixing window latches, repairing leaky faucets, replacing furnace filters and smoke alarm batteries, installing lightbulbs in hard-to-reach places, and getting supplies at the hardware store. Keep a running list of things he needs. Oftentimes, this strategy works better than giving your husband a "Honey-Do list," which can ruin his weekend as well as your own.

- *Hire a techno-geek for electronic jobs.* A high school or college student can hook up your computer, TV, VCR, cable, or stereo. Electronic tasks can take hours of your time and a few minutes of theirs.

- *Hire experts.* In minutes, experts can do what would take you hours to do. Travel agents, accountants, landscape designers, and painters have skills that can simplify your life. Also, many professionals can buy supplies at a reduced cost, which can help you afford their services. Balance your time and talents against the cost of hiring experts.

- *Inspire your husband.* Many working women complicate their lives by doing too much while their husbands do too little. If this describes you, back off a few notches. Then read Cris's book, *The Givers and the Takers.*

- *Require more help from the kids.* They have more energy than you do. Harness it. Teach them valuable life skills.

Errand Simplifiers

Racing around in a car is draining. You probably no longer view errands as a pastime and would rather spend time doing other things. To simplify your life, reduce your errand load. Many errands can wait and some may be eliminated. Run less and live more.

Make a red check mark by tips that will simplify errand running.

❏ **Do more by phone, fax, and mail.**

- Shopping by catalogue for kids' clothes, gifts, and office supplies has become a savior for busy people. Products can be ordered 24 hours a day. Tear out the pages you need and recycle the rest of the catalogue.
- Mail your film to a photo developing service. Save two trips.
- Mail items that need to be repaired (such as eyeglasses) and have them mailed back. Save two more trips!

❏ **To save time, order online.**
With the advent of the Internet, more and more products—such as CDs, books, clothing, and computer software—are becoming available online. Ordering online will become more popular as people feel secure about using their credit cards. If you are concerned about security, get a credit card for online purchases only.

❏ **Discover Peapod.**
Peapod is an online—www.peapod.com—grocery shopping and delivery service. Once you enroll, you can order groceries online or by fax. Your groceries will be delivered within 24 hours. Peapod is a flexible program that charges by the month and/or the delivery. Set up a standing grocery list and add or delete items each time you order. Peapod is currently available in the metropolitan areas of Chicago, Boston, Dallas, Austin, Houston, Columbus, San Jose, and San Francisco. New cities are continually being added.

❏ **Spend less time schlepping mail to the post office.**

- Get an account with FedEx or UPS. Let them pick up your mail.
- Get Priority Mail pouches and $3 stamps from the post of-

fice. For $3 you can send anything (any weight) that fits into the cardboard pouch. Your pouch will be delivered in two days.

- Buy a postage scale and get a mail rate chart from the post office. Buy stamps of varying amounts and save yourself a trip to the post office.
- Stock manila envelopes and padded mailing envelopes in varying sizes, so you can mail a package of any size easily. Recycle envelopes you receive from others.

❏ **Simplify your life by making lists.**
Cris's friend Jacqueline says, "I have daily lists, long-range lists, gift lists, grocery lists, drugstore lists, and lists of movies I want to rent. My husband, Henry, often asks me to be sure to put him on a list."

- *Make a "Three-Part list."* Divide your trusty daily To Do list into three parts—To Call, To Do—In, and To Do—Out.
- *Create permanent lists.* Create permanent lists for groceries, then check items as you run out. You could create a Farmer's Market list and a Costco list.
- *Refer to your To Do—Out list (errands list) while you chauffeur the kids.* People who frequently chauffeur children have small pockets of time in between drop-offs and pickups. In the morning, determine which errands you can do before, during, and after chauffeuring.
- *Use Post-it notes along with your To Do list.* Put a task to be done or a person to call on a Post-it note. Move the note from day to day, or week to week, on your calendar until it gets done. It saves writing and rewriting on your To Do list.

❏ **Carry personal information cards.**
In addition to a business card, it's nice to have a personal card with your name, address, phone/fax numbers, and e-mail address. Give your personal card to new friends and acquaintances. Hand it to store clerks when you want something held

or ordered. Give it to people who need your address to send you something.

❏ Keep claim checks with you.
Carry these items in your date book. You will always have them when you need them and you will always know where they are.

❏ Make remembering easier.
To remember things more easily, stick a Post-it on your exit door. If you need to have something repaired, put it in your car the night before. Jim sticks things to be remembered in his shoes. Sandra puts them in her underwear drawer. When Judy makes a dish for a potluck dinner, she remembers to take it by putting her keys on top of the dish.

❏ For Serious Simplifiers only!
Run errands *just one day a week*. Designate a particular day and write it on your calendar. Obviously, some errands are urgent and cannot wait for Errand Day. Learn to discern the difference between urgent and non-urgent errands. To run fewer errands, look for the underlying reasons behind your errands. Then eliminate the reasons!

∽

I have no time to be in a hurry.

—Henry David Thoreau

DAY 20

Be Mindful, Savor Time

Task: *Today, practice living in the present—not in fast forward or reverse. Do one mundane job with your full attention. When you pay attention in your daily life, whatever you do becomes transformed.*

Step 1. Sit still for a few minutes before beginning the next activity on your To Do list. Focus on your breathing. When you feel calm, centered, and grounded, turn your attention to your task. Next, walk slowly to the site of your task.

Step 2. Now do the job slowly and deliberately. Perform this act as if it were your last.

Step 3. When mental and physical distractions arise, remind yourself to refocus. If the interruption is about something you must do later—such as calling the plumber— write it down and return to your chore.

Moments can seem short or long according to our perception of them. Busy moments seem to pass quickly and relaxed moments seem to pass slowly. For example, if you frantically run errands, beginning at nine in the morning, it will be noon before you know it. But if you watch a clock tick for an hour, time will drag on and on.

Have you ever heard people say: "It's June, and it seems like it was just Christmas" or "I just got out of high school and now

I'm forty-three." The true length of our lives is determined by how we perceive time.

Time seems to pass slowly when we wait in lines. Many people resent waiting in banks, post offices, and doctors' offices. Instead of fretting, *meditate while you wait.*

Today Is Ecstasy!

Yesterday is history. Tomorrow is a mystery. Today is ecstasy! Tony Robbins says, "Live every day with an attitude of gratitude." How often do we do that? Most of us spend far too much time fantasizing about the future and reminiscing about the past. Instead of being present, we look elsewhere for happiness. Come up with a few creative ways to be more present. Here are some suggestions:

- *Notice the sun and wind.* Feel the effects of the sun and wind on your skin and on the leaves of trees.
- *Listen for animal noises.* Crickets make one of the loudest sounds on earth and we rarely hear them because our mind chatter is so loud.
- *Look at mundane objects longer.* While walking, we tend to glance at objects for a split second. The external world is a blur. Learn to look at objects for five seconds or longer.
- *Say the names of things.* Become fully present by saying the names of things you normally see for a split second. Say "oak," "gardenia," "sparrow," and "picket fence."
- *Do repetitive acts slowly.* Cris uses check writing to bring herself into the present. She writes her checks slowly.
- *Eat with your left hand (if you are right-handed).* You will eat more slowly or your food will end up in your lap.
- *Watch kids.* They swing, slide, skip, jump, and laugh more than adults. Take a cue from them.
- *Meditate to feel great.* Anytime you are fully present, you are meditating. Meditation is full concentration on one object or activity. To explore meditation, read Eknath Eas-

waran's book, *Meditation—A Simple Eight-Point Program for Translating Spiritual Ideals into Daily Life.*

Time Goes down the Tube

By the time the average person is 65 years old, he has watched nine years of television, according to *Health* magazine. Cris and her husband, Dave, weaned themselves from TV while they were on a three-week voyage on the Burgundy Canal in France.

"Picture us driving down a flooded street in a Winnebago," says Cris. "That's how we looked in our canal boat. During our trip, we noticed we felt better without television. Our evenings were quieter. We read, took walks, wrote postcards, and played Backgammon. We met new friends and swapped stories. Back at home, we traded our new twenty-seven-inch television for our son's thirteen-inch model. We keep the small television in a closet and bring it out for biographies, rented movies, and special documentaries. We reduced our viewing time by ninety percent."

To simplify TV watching, Cris signed up for public television's online highlights via e-mail. If this idea appeals to you, go to www.pbs.org—and then click on "PBS Previews." Enjoy!

Reclaim your life from television. Be careful what you feed your soul.

Time Simplifiers

Learn to savor the moment. Ram Dass said, "What you fear and want is in the future; what you regret is in the past; what you have is here—right now."

Make a red check mark by tips that will help you manage time.

❑ **Don't get it right, get it written.**
Know the difference between what you need to do and what you would like to do if you had unlimited time. We wrote this

book in nine months and could have spent twenty years on it.
We learned to *freeze the design*.

❏ **Avoid waiting in long lines.**
Do your grocery shopping when other people are eating sup-
per. Don't do your banking on Friday afternoons; bank by mail.
When you find yourself in a long line, note the time.

❏ **Schedule downtime between activities.**
Downtime enables you to reflect on your last activity and prepare for the next.

❏ **Work in blocks of time.**
"I've worked all day and have nothing to show for it! I'm exhausted." Sound familiar? You feel unsuccessful because you
did a lot of small, unrelated chores. To feel more accomplished:

- Set aside large chunks of time (3–4 hours) for important
  projects.
- Allot adequate time for routine chores. Be realistic about
  how long it takes to do chores. For example, dinner might
  take from five to seven o'clock to prepare, serve, eat, and
  clean up.
- Place a higher value on routine chores—such as grooming,
  straightening the house, going to the dentist—and allow
  enough time to complete them. Resentment leads to fatigue.

❏ **Make more standing appointments.**
Deciding whether to do something is more time consuming than
making commitments and sticking to them.

- *Appointments with others*. Make standing appointments
  for anything you do on an ongoing basis.
- *Appointments with yourself*. Our mothers used to wash on
  Mondays, grocery shop on Tuesdays, and clean the house
  on Wednesdays. Follow their example and assign specific
  days to your major tasks.

❏ **Use your prime time for your hardest tasks.**
Are you a morning, afternoon, or midnight person? Your prime time is when you have the most energy. Do your hardest tasks, the ones that require the most concentration, during your prime time. Move your more mundane tasks to your low energy time of day.

❏ **Spend less time on mundane duties.**

- Buy a postage scale and stamps in three denominations—for letters, postcards, and extra ounces. (Our friend Jennifer orders stamps by mail.) Electronic scales, which sell for about $75, show the weight of a letter or package as well as the first, third, and international air postage costs.
- Take the first doctor's appointment in the morning before she gets off schedule because of emergencies and people who are late.
- To get a prescription filled, you normally drop it off and pick it up. Have your doctor call in the prescription and save a trip. Use a mail-order pharmacy such as Women's International Pharmacy at 800-279-5708 and make no trips at all.
- Have your dry cleaning picked up and delivered. Or better yet, wear washable clothing.

❏ **Get public television previews by e-mail.**
On the Internet, go to www.pbs.org.

❏ **For Serious Simplifiers only!**
Sign up for a week-long retreat that requires you to be silent. A week of silence will be one of the most renewing weeks of your life.

◢◣

Most people pursue pleasure with such breathless haste they hurry right past it.

—Søren Kierkegaard

Travel Light in Style

Task: *Set up a Travel Center today. Include travel lists, travel documents, travel accessories, frequent flyer information, travel destination files, and books on travel. Complete instructions follow.*

Last year, when Connie was traveling, she wrote in her diary, "Traveling is complicated. It's so hard to get out of the house. By the time we leave, we are worn out. When we return, there's so much catching up to do. So why do we travel?

"I travel because I want to break my routine and leave my To Do list behind. I like experiencing a different pace and style of life. For the past 18 days, I have traveled with a purse and one small suitcase. What freedom!"

Indeed, traveling offers us an opportunity to practice living simply. To make traveling a no-brainer, set up a Travel Center, which will enable you to leave home without becoming exhausted by the exiting process.

Set Up a Travel Center

Put travel phone numbers in one place

When you make reservations, you will have all of the numbers you need in one place under "Travel"—on a Rolodex card, in your address book, or in a Palm Pilot. Include the following numbers:

- Airlines' phone numbers
- Frequent flyer numbers
- Airline lounge membership numbers
- Passport numbers
- Credit card numbers
- Travel agent's number

Make permanent travel lists

Even the most brilliant mind cannot compete with the trusty list. Keep several travel lists and forms on your computer or make several copies.

Packing Lists: Create a master packing list and specialized lists for ski trips, hiking trips, beach trips, and foreign travel trips. When you are finished packing, check your lists for forgotten items.

Things-to-Do-Before-Leaving List: This list has reminders—like set the timers, clean out the refrigerator, and get a dog sitter. Make a list of people, with their phone numbers, to call before leaving—the police, post office (to stop mail), alarm company, newspaper, neighbors, dog kennel, plant-waterer, and people who need to know you will be gone.

Household Instructions Form: This form contains house sitter and baby-sitter information. It has the address and location of your house for the fire department and repair people, and a map of the vital organs of the house, such as the gas shut-off valve and water main. It lists phone numbers for neighbors, repair people, the vet, your children's teachers and friends, and people who come to the house on a regular basis.

Household Operations List: This list explains how things work—the phones, the sprinklers, the automatic lights, and the burglar alarm. Include a sketch of your house, showing the location of these things, for a house sitter.

Medical Release Form: Create a form with medical release information. Include your child's name, the doctor's name and phone number, and your signature. This medical release form is ready to go after adding the dates you will be gone and the child sitter's name.

Create a Travel Accessories Center

In one location, put your travel folder, which holds your tickets, passport, itineraries, airline frequent flyer cards, and airport lounge cards. In this area, store earplugs, eyeshades, neck pillow, lint brush, travel-size tissues, shoe bags, and various bags for packing small items like jewelry, stockings, and underwear. Plastic Ziploc bags are great for these items.

Set up the following travel file folders:

Frequent Flyer Miles. This folder contains mileage statements, awards brochures, and vouchers. Be sure to clean out the old mileage statements and old brochures each time you add new ones, so you only have the current information.

Upcoming Trip. As soon as you decide to take a trip, make a folder for it, such as "Paris: July 1–8, 2000." In the folder, put your plane reservations, hotel accommodations, airline tickets, articles about restaurants and things to do, and miscellaneous information. Print out your Travel Lists (above) and place them in the folder. Take the folder on your trip and use it to store reminders—names of people you meet and brochures of places you visit.

Trips I Have Taken. Keep files from past trips, labeled by place and date. In these files, keep information that brings back memories and that enables you to pass on names of hotels, restaurants, or interesting information to friends. When you return from a trip, the file is already created, because you had the folder with you. (See preceding tip.)

Trips I Dream of Taking. These files are great, but don't let them grow unchecked. Travel agents, travel book writers, and the World Wide Web accumulate travel information for you as well.

Create a travel library

To find your travel books quickly, collect them in one area of your bookshelf. Since travel books have a shelf life, recycle them when they become outdated.

What to Pack

Take no more than a week's worth of clothing. The longer the trip, the less you should take. Going to Laundromats can be part of the adventure. Also, beware of last-minute additions to your luggage. It is not unusual to meticulously plan clothing for a trip and then impulsively grab five more items. When packing, consider these ideas:

Pack clothes that layer well: Jackets, sweaters, T-shirts, and undershirts are the elements of layering. Temperatures change, so bring clothing that layer.

Go for two or three solid colors—not patterns: Prints are limiting. Choose two or three basic colors, then add color with accessories.

Add accessories for variety: A few lightweight accessories can make a boring wardrobe come to life. A unique belt buckle, smashing scarf, and exotic pin take up little space.

Plan a trip with two pairs of earrings: Wear a daytime pair and take a pair for evening wear. Worry less about theft.

Bring just two pairs of shoes: Light travelers take two pairs of comfortable low-heeled shoes—and they don't break in a new pair of walking shoes.

Pack dressy and business clothing in dry-cleaner bags: Clothes packed in dry-cleaner bags (or tissue) don't tend to wrinkle. Hang bagged clothes as soon as you reach your destination.

Buy exotic clothes at outdoor markets: Pack lightly and purchase a few inexpensive native fashions on the road. Clothes make wonderful remembrances.

Bring your swimsuit: Always pack a swimsuit and be prepared to take advantage of unexpected pools, Jacuzzis, hot tubs, and hot springs.

Pack what you can comfortably carry for a mile: You may have to walk a long distance to catch a bus, change planes, or find a camel-for-hire. Test the weight of your bag by carrying it for a block.

Travel Simplifiers

Traveling can be simple. Wherever you go, you own nothing, except the clothes on your back and in your bag. Your job, car, house, mail, phone, and relationships are left behind. Life is simpler on the road.

Make a red check mark by tips that will simplify travel.

❏ **Know which bags are best for traveling light.**
The 45-inch (overall dimensions) carry-on style bag is best. This size can be stowed in overhead bins. (Cris often travels with a backpack.) In addition to a primary suitcase, you may carry on another good-sized bag, usually a shoulder tote, that fits under the seat. Avoid heavy garment bags. Though useful for hanging clothes, hanging storage is not always available. You may need a luggage cart if it is packed too full.

❏ **Keep a toiletry kit ready to go.**
Restock your kit each time you return from a trip. Bring one kind of soap for your hair, body, and laundry. Share toiletries with your traveling companion.

❏ **Avoid lost luggage.**

- Remove old destination tags, the number one cause of lost luggage. Don't confuse baggage handlers with several routing tags.
- Tie a brightly colored ribbon or piece of yarn onto the handle of your bag to quickly identify your checked-in luggage on the baggage carousel.

❏ **Bring a laundry bag.**
To keep your suitcase organized, pack a drawstring laundry bag. Keep clean clothes separated from dirty ones.

❏ **Send unneeded items home.**

- Midway through your trip, send home a box of unneeded things (souvenirs, extra clothing). Some hotels have a package-mailing service. If you buy from a reputable store, let the shop ship it.
- Mail home museum brochures, menus, small souvenirs, postcards, tax receipts, and used maps. Bring a few manila envelopes for this purpose. Why carry maps of Italy to Sweden by train?

❏ **Don't bring a travel iron.**
Deal with wrinkles by hanging your clothes in the bathroom and taking a steamy shower—the heat and moisture relax wrinkles. Or ask to borrow an iron at the hotel. To avoid wrinkles, place tissue, recycled plastic bags, or small items—like socks, undies, scarves—into the folds of your clothes.

❏ **Leave your valuables at home.**
If you don't bring valuables, you won't have to lock your luggage or worry about leaving them in hotel rooms. Pack things you don't mind losing.

❏ **Don't bring the camera on every trip.**
We know a sophisticated couple who travel internationally several times a year. Their mutual decision was to leave the camera home. Instead, they purchase the nicest postcards available and add the date of their trip to each one. In fifteen years of traveling, they have never regretted this decision.

❏ **Fly in comfort.**

- Bring a pair of socks or slippers so you can take off your shoes on the plane. Wear comfortable clothes such as pants with an elasticized waistband. For sleeping, bring earplugs, eye-covers, and a blow-up neck pillow.

- Locate seats with extra leg room. Request a bulkhead seat or sit in an exit row.

❏ **Stay moist.**

- Apply moisturizers and lip balm during the flight. Pressurized cabins are dry, dehydrating climates. Drink at least eight ounces of water for every hour in the air. Avoid alcohol—it's dehydrating!
- Pack juicy fruits and vegetables. Slices of apples, melons, oranges, celery, carrots, tomatoes, and cucumbers are great to eat in-flight because they are full of water.

❏ **For Serious Simplifiers only!**
Travel with carry-on luggage and skip the lines at the airport. Make a drop-dead short packing list and stick to it! Light travelers are free and independent.

～

Simplicity is a journey, not a destination. Enjoy the trek!

DAY 22

Keep Track of Your Valuables

Task: *Today, create a Valuables Binder for art, jewelry, silverware, and collections of anything you value and worry about losing to fire and theft. Detailed instructions follow.*

If you have valuables, be willing to list them—and then enjoy them without worrying. Enjoy your silver. Don't hide it. Drink from your crystal wine glasses. Don't dust them. If your valuables make you feel vulnerable and are a burden, pass them on.

What follows are suggestions for keeping track of your costly possessions so you can be compensated for them in case of fire or theft. These records may also be used when you sell or donate items.

1. *Create a Valuables Binder:* Make a binder with dividers and clear sheet protectors. Label the spine. List everything you consider a valuable. (If making a binder is too much trouble, create a file folder instead.)
2. *Photograph your valuables.* Gather up your valuables and photograph them in one session. Be sure to date the photos. *Videotaping* is an alternative to photographing. With your camera, *talk* your way around the house. Date the video. (If this seems formidable, contact your insurance company for professionals who document possessions.)
3. *Include receipts.* Find the sales receipts for your valuable

possessions and put them into the sheet protector pages of your binder.

4. *Gather up appraisals and authentication documents.* Put these documents in your binder.

5. *Store your Valuables Binder in a safe place.* Keep it where flames and sticky fingers can't reach it. You might store it in a home safe or a safe-deposit box. If it is inaccessible, make a copy to keep at home. This binder contains essential data for processing an insurance claim. Keep it up to date.

As you ponder each item, ask yourself, "How much happiness does this item bring me? How much work?" When all is said and done, the benefits of ownership should far outweigh the drawbacks.

Only you know how much your valuables mean to you.

What Happened to David's Valuables

In 1988, David Dickinson sold his dental practice and put all of his possessions in a 20 by 30–foot storage space in a large building in downtown San Diego. He stored his furniture, antiques, original artwork, 2,000 books, a tractor lawn mower, his boat's sails, and enough dental equipment to open another practice.

"I had so much stuff that a friend referred to it as The Mountain," he told us. "I stored it so I could travel. Between trips to the British West Indies, Brazil, Europe, and the South Pacific, I lived aboard my thirty-eight–foot sailboat, *Jaga*, in a slip at the Marriott Hotel and Marina, a few blocks from my possessions.

"One afternoon, a friend called to say, 'Your storage unit is on fire.' I ran to the scene and watched helplessly as my stuff fueled a huge fire. It was the largest fire in San Diego County in fifty years; it consumed an entire block of buildings.

"Five days later, I received permission to sort through the rubble. Nothing was salvageable. How did I feel? Frankly, I felt a sense of loss mixed with a sense of *relief.*

"The fire made me realize that those things had been a burden. For many years, I had worried about, moved, and set up that stuff. I was not emotionally devastated because my life was not centered on possessions. I have always felt my most valuable asset, my greatest gift, is life itself.

"Because the building was high risk, my possessions were uninsured. I received very little money from the class action suit and lost about $300,000.

"What did I learn?

"I learned that losing everything in a fire is insignificant. When people lose body parts, a loved one, a family member, or even a pet, it's a far greater loss."

Valuable Simplifiers

If you own valuables, you must be willing to lose them, just like everything else in life. What follows are a few precautionary steps you can take to secure your valuables.

Make a red check mark by tips that simplify owning valuables.

❏ **Get a safe and feel secure.**
A safe can simplify your life by creating a secure place for small valuables. Stash jewelry, passports, plane tickets, and other precious commodities. A safe is also an excellent place to keep cash for emergencies such as earthquakes and other unexpected disasters.

❏ **Secure your valuables before you leave town.**
Before you leave your house for an extended period of time, box up some of your valuables and put them with dead storage in the garage or basement. Why tempt burglars.

❏ **List the contents of your safe-deposit box.**
Store the list with the key. It's easy to forget which stock certificates, title documents, and other important papers are stored in

the box. By keeping a running list with dates of deposit, you will know what you have—save trips to the bank.

❏ For Serious Simplifiers only!

Scan your house and ask, "Which valuables bring little enjoyment and much distress?" After you have identified these items, sell them or give them to relatives who will enjoy them more. If you are serious about simplifying, break your attachment to things you worry about losing. Being free of concerns about possessions simplifies life.

∽

Serious Simplifiers would rather hike in the woods than catalogue their goods.

DAY 23

Give Vanishing Gifts

Task: *Today, tackle your wrapping paper, ribbons, gift bags, and gift tags/cards. Save a few of your favorite rolls of paper, some matching ribbon, and some gift-enclosure cards. Give away your extraneous wrapping supplies (give a few rolls to the kids). If you cannot bear to give away beautiful wrapping paper, store the excess out of sight. Simplicity is about using up what you have—and keeping things flowing through your life!*

Gift giving is about saying you care. Gifts are symbols of love and appreciation. But giving gifts is risky business. It is easy to give inappropriate gifts, or gifts that become garage sales items. So what's the solution? *Give consumable gifts:* Gifts that don't clutter people's lives. Gifts guaranteed *not* to last a lifetime!

Give gifts that are truly consumable

- *Gourmet foods.* Jams, jellies, pastas, pestos, vinegars, flavored oils, and sun-dried tomatoes make great gifts. Many gourmet foods come beautifully packaged.
- *Local wines.* How about a Merlot, rich with the scents of the harvest, or a crisp Muscadet? A sparkling Burgundy? A Zinfandel? Select sulfite-free organic wines.
- *Fresh flowers.* A bouquet is a phone call away. A beautiful selection of fresh flowers is always welcomed. (Men

love them, too.) A Christmas wreath is a perfect holiday gift.

- *Toiletries.* Give scented soaps, silky hand lotions, bath and body oils. Bath salts are always appreciated. Avoid perfumes. Most women have more than they can use in a lifetime.

Give an opportunity to do something special

- *Experiences.* Plan a special outing to celebrate a friend's birthday. Arrange a picnic, a hike in the mountains, a walk along a beach, a dinner, a play, or a movie. Our friend Lynn gave her hairstylist a zoo membership so she can take her two kids for brief visits without paying an entrance fee.
- *Gift certificates.* Buy a certificate for a facial, massage, pedicure, or a day at a spa, dinner at a restaurant, or an overnight at a bed-and-breakfast. Also give concert, cinema, theater, and sports-events tickets. To save time, order these gifts by phone—"Here's my credit card number, please send me a gift certificate for a river rafting trip down the Rogue."

Use your talents to create a gift

- *Photos of a festivity.* Our friend Jeannine says, "When I attend a special celebration, I take photos and send them to the hostess as a thank-you. Give a stack of photos or a book of photos or a single snapshot, enlarged and framed, of an event you attended."
- *Homemade computer stationery.* If you own a computer and color printer and enjoy experimenting, create a dozen sheets of personal stationery. Most office supply stores stock attractive recycled papers with matching envelopes.
- *Services.* Volunteer your talent as a sitter (tot sitter, teen sitter, parent sitter, pet sitter, house sitter), typist, file clerk, researcher, organizer, shopper, photographer, lawn mower, veggie garden planter, room painter, window washer, caterer, cake baker, car detailer, dog trainer, computer whiz,

or tennis pro. Or, if you're flush and pressed for time, hire a professional to serve your friend.

Use gifts to introduce your friends to new concepts

- *Eco-Products Basket.* Many people are unfamiliar with non-toxic products. Introduce them to your friends by creating gift baskets full of eco-gifts for the kitchen, bathroom, and laundry room. Include a shower filter—few people have them. Buy products from an environmental catalogue or your local health food store.
- *Full-spectrum lightbulbs.* Many people do not know that full-spectrum lightbulbs duplicate the characteristics of natural lighting, reduce eye stress, and create a pleasing, relaxing, warmly colored ambiance. Sources for full-spectrum bulbs are Frontgate catalogue at (800) 626-6488 and www.realgoods.com.
- *Tapes, books, and magazines.* Connie gives motivational tapes and asks her friends to pass them on. Cris inscribes books with, "Enjoy this book and pass it on to a friend." Magazine subscriptions and special-interest newsletters also make excellent gifts.

Give the gift of charity

- *Charitable donations.* Make a charitable donation in the name of a friend or family member. This is a great gift for people who truly don't want one more thing in their life, but would be honored by a gift to a nonprofit organization. Share your values with children by making a contribution in their honor. For instance, give a tree in their name.

Give people an opportunity to choose their own gift

- *Catalogue shopping.* We know a grandmother who sends her grandchild the J. Crew catalogue with a self-addressed stamped envelope and a note that says, "For your birthday, circle something you would like and send me the page." Catalogue companies simplify life because they wrap and deliver gifts.

Gift-Giving Simplifiers

Look forward to gift giving. Think of ways to maximize the joy and minimize the stress. And most important, do it your way.

Make a red check mark by tips that will simplify gift giving.

❏ **Rethink gifts.**

- *Don't feel obligated to give gifts.* Sometimes a card, a phone call, or a visit is enough.
- *Don't feel obligated to keep gifts.* Return unwanted gifts immediately. It's better to get cash or credit than live with an irritant. Unwanted gifts can be a major source of clutter.
- *Don't feel obligated to give gifts to your spouse's family.* Women often complain about having to buy gifts for their husband's family. If you feel that way, don't do it. Send a card and focus your energy on your own family's traditions. Your husband will work it out with his kin. Simplify!

❏ **Give the same gift to everybody.**
Giving the same present to friends and family is a great way to share your favorite products, which are often cheaper by the dozen. Who's going to complain about receiving a great CD or a fabulous bottle of wine?

❏ **Create a signature wrap.**
Create *one* terrific look for wrapping gifts. All you need is a roll of wrapping paper with matching ribbon. One wrap can be for adults, another for kids. When you use it up, create a fresh, new look. Eliminate those chaotic baskets full of wrapping papers and mismatched ribbons. Ideas for signature wraps: Brown paper tied with raffia. Sunday comics for kids' gifts. Gift bags in

one color, and several sizes, with complementary tissue for spilling out the top. *Go for one look and use it up.*

❏ **Let the store wrap it and mail it.**
Many shops wrap and send gifts. If you have them sent out of state, you will not be charged tax. Use gift-wrap services whenever available.

❏ **For Serious Simplifiers only!**
Give far fewer gifts and far more hugs. Gifts are symbols of love.

∽

Give gifts with a short shelf life.

Create Hassle-Free Holidays

Task: *Make a list of the holidays you celebrate annually. Beside each entry, write down what each holiday means to you. For example, Thanksgiving may mean organizing a big potluck dinner for friends who don't have anyplace else to go. Next, make another list of holidays with columns entitled "Joyful Activities" and "Stressful Activities." Fill in the blanks. For example, a joyful Christmas activity might be "Sending cards," whereas a stressful activity might be "Finding perfect gifts for household help." Once the list is made, vow to maximize joy and minimize stress.*

Holidays are celebrations—festive occasions for sharing food, music, and laughter with family and friends. Celebrating holidays can be both joyful and stressful. Look for ways to keep the joy and let go of the stress.

Bring more mirth, warmth, and friendship to your holidays. Savor the food, decorations, celebrations, and gift giving and vow to make your holidays less stressful. By "holidays," we don't just mean Christmas. Holidays include Thanksgiving, Valentine's Day, birthdays, Halloween, Easter, Passover, July Fourth, Jewish High Holidays, Memorial Day, Labor Day, and any other holiday that you celebrate.

To simplify holidays, celebrate them when *you feel like it* and ignore them when you don't. Don't feel pressured by the media, merchants, friends, relatives, and age-old traditions. Orchestrating and participating in holiday activities is not mandatory. On the other hand, if you want to plan a great holiday party with clever invitations, fabulous food, and thoughtful gifts, make it a joyful project. Be true to yourself.

Live authentically. Honor your feelings about the holidays. You may find that you enjoy Thanksgiving but not Halloween. Or you may like Halloween but dread New Year's Eve.

Holidays can be a wonderful outlet for your creative side. The most demanding holiday tends to be Christmas, which is often a stressful mix of family intimacy and frantic shopping. Ask, "How can I simplify Christmas? This year, what can I do differently to make it more enjoyable?" Here are some ways our friends simplify:

Put ornaments and colorful lights on a large house plant.

Give jars of gourmet jam as a thank-you to service people.

Go away for the holidays as a family present to each other.

Buy a plastic Christmas tree, store it with the lights on it, and be ready for next year.

Holiday Simplifiers

Think of ways to simplify the holidays. How can you do less and still achieve the results you desire?

Make a red check mark by tips that will simplify the holidays.

❏ **Think grand decorations—not teeny.**
Large holiday decorations are easier to set up and put away than miniatures—and they make a powerful statement. *Simplicity is about having more large things and fewer small things.*

❏ **Simplify Christmas cards.**

- It's not necessary to send Christmas cards to everybody in your address book. Instead, use them for keeping in touch with people you rarely see.

- E-mail your Christmas message to friends online.
- Network with cards—include a flyer about your business or favorite cause.
- Color copy a recent photograph and use it as your Christmas card.
- Create a scrapbook or binder of your family's annual Christmas card. Once you have made it, adding a new card takes seconds. (Cris pastes her Christmas newsletter on the first page of her yearly scrapbook. She uses her scrapbook to delete mementos from her bulletin board.)
- Frame your Christmas cards. Lois hangs her family Christmas photo cards in her hallway. It is fun to see how her family members have changed over the years.

❑ Recycle Christmas decorations.
Next Christmas, notice which decorations you enjoy and which are left in the box. Give your neglected, forsaken ornaments and decorations to a more loving home.

❑ Keep a set of greeting cards handy.
Make fewer trips to the card store. Keep cards on hand for birthdays, get wells, thank-yous, and congratulations. For versatility, stock attractive blank cards and write your own greeting. Be on the cutting edge and send online greeting cards from www.bluemountain.com. They are free.

❑ Make postcards out of greeting cards.
Re-use the greeting cards you receive. Cut off the front of the card and stamp the back. Create a basketful of pre-stamped postcards. Dash off a note in seconds.

❑ List birthdays by month in your date book.
Make it easy to remember birthdays. Place a birthday list at the beginning of each month in your date book. On the list, note what you would like to do for each person.

❑ Collect creative ideas.
Make a binder with clear sheet protectors (or a file folder) for

creative things you have seen that inspire you. Include flyers, brochures, party invitations, Christmas card ideas. Remember to keep tossing less interesting or repetitive samples as you add new ones.

❏ **Create a personal portfolio.**
If you create cards or art for holidays or parties, keep a folder or binder of the art for future reference. Designating a binder or a folder gets these priceless creations out of the drawers, off the bookshelves and desktop, and into one place where they can be enjoyed or referred to. We each have a binder with our computer art.

❏ **For Serious Simplifiers only!**
For one year, as each holiday approaches, choose *one* celebratory activity. For example, for Christmas, just send cards, or make a wreath, or decorate a tree. Fully experience one aspect of each holiday—and ignore your least-favorite holidays completely. To simplify gift giving for one year, give the same gift to everyone on your list or send a card. Get out of the loop for a year.

∽

I have just three things to teach: simplicity, patience, and compassion. These three are your greatest treasures.

—Lao-tzu

DAY 25

Enjoy Your Photos and Mementos

Task: *Today, round up all of your photos and put them in one place. That's all you have to do. Make a commitment to buy some photo boxes in the near future. With these boxes, you will be able to sort your photos. Read on for the details.*

Knowing you have photos of your past and your ancestors' past is comforting, but having to rummage through drawers, shoe boxes, and grocery bags to find a particular photo isn't. Get control of your photos by creating a simple system with easy steps.

Simplicity is about living more in the present and less in the past and future. The present is full of sensory experiences that you can feel, taste, and smell. The past is composed of hazy, faded memories of bygone days, and the future is full of wistful illusions.

When you think about your photographs, here are some questions you might ask yourself: How many reminders of the past should I keep? What will be the present price of preserving the past? How can I commemorate the past and still live fully in the present?

Tackle your photos in bite-sized pieces.

Organize Your Photos from the Past

Step 1. Round up all your photos.
(This is today's task at the top of the page.) Collecting your photos in one place is a big step in the right direction.

Step 2. Purchase several sturdy cardboard photo filing boxes.
Inexpensive photo filing boxes are available in photo shops, discount stores, and office supply stores. These boxes enable you to store photos in a uniform manner. Buy plenty of boxes and avoid making several trips to the store. One of the basic tenets of organizing is having enough supplies to do a job without running out.

Step 3. Sort your photos.
Categorize them by person, event, year, or "era"—when you lived on Oak Street, when the girls were babies, before you moved to Colorado. Label the boxes. You may find that sorting by the academic calendar, September 1–August 31, makes more sense than sorting by the calendar year.

Step 4. Put the photos into the labeled boxes.
Remember, you are not an archivist for the Smithsonian. It is better to box up your photos imperfectly than not at all. When you have time, you may go back and perfect your system. Or not!

Step 5. Buy several inexpensive, easy-to-use photo albums.
Inexpensive albums enable you to quickly display photos without having to debate the fate of each one—"Should I keep it, trim it, or toss it?" The albums we like hold photos horizontally and vertically.

Step 6. Put the photos in the albums one box at a time.
You can do this in one-hour sittings while watching TV, sipping coffee, or playing music. It's amazing how little time it takes to empty one box of photos.

Step 7. Don't worry about negatives.
You probably have bunches of old negatives. Put them all together and label them as well as you can. For example, one bunch might say, "1975–1985." Put them in a fireproof place. (You can store them in a personal safe, in a media storage vault, or with companies like Datasafe, which store documents.) If your house burns and you lose your photos, you can include the printing of your negatives on your insurance claim.

Organize Your Most Recent Photos

You don't have to organize your old photos before tackling the ones you have just taken. The goal is to get your latest photos out of their envelopes and into the hands of people who will enjoy them.

Step 1. Purchase several sturdy cardboard photograph filing boxes.
Refer to Step 2 on page 157 for doing this task.

Step 2. Buy some inexpensive, easy-to-use photo albums.
(See Step 5 above.) Find a way to purchase albums by the case. They are cheaper by the dozen.

Step 3. Put your recent photos in an album.
As soon as you pick up your photos from the developer, slip them into an album—not into a junk drawer. Enjoy them immediately.

Step 4. Store recent negatives and duplicates in one photo box.
Start a new photo box each year. Label the negatives by date and/or event and store them with the duplicates. Look in this box to find photos to frame or send to friends. At the end of the year, take the negatives to a fire-safe location.

Simple Ways to Enjoy Photos

- *Make postcards and greeting cards.* To make postcards, paste photos onto card stock—old file folders work well. This is a clever way to use duplicate photos or photos that are not quite "album quality." To make greeting cards, fold card stock in half and paste a photo on the front.
- *Create a yearly collage.* Make a collage of your ten best photos of the year. Frame it and hang it for everyone to enjoy.
- *Capture each birthday.* Take photos of your child on each

birthday and add them to a birthday album. Jeannine takes a black-and-white photo of her daughters on their birthdays each year. She selects the best photo, frames it, and hangs it in her library with photos from previous birthdays.

- *Create a changing gallery.* Keep several framed photos of recent trips, portraits, and activities in a well-traveled place in your house. Change the photos in the frames periodically.
- *Enlarge an unforgettable experience.* Capture an "unforgettable experience," enlarge it, elegantly frame it, and hang it in a wonderful location.
- *Make photographic quality reprints from old photographs.* Kodak manufactures a machine that makes good quality reprints on photographic paper from old and new photos. You don't need a negative. Photos can be reduced and enlarged. Look for these machines in camera stores.
- *Put Christmas photos from friends in your photo album.* What do you do with photos you receive from friends during the holidays? Why not insert them into your photo album with your holiday photos?

Color Copiers Are Fun!

Instantly duplicate, reduce, and enlarge your photos on a color copy machine. Below are a few creative things you can do with color copies.

- *Greeting cards:* Copy a photo onto the bottom half of a piece of card stock. Fold the paper in half and you will have a greeting card.
- *Posters:* Enlarge photos on 11 × 17–inch paper and back with foam-core. Posters make inexpensive gifts.
- *Collage:* Create a collage of photos by copying several photos onto one sheet. Crop or overlap photos as necessary. Making a collage of multiple photos is simpler than

making copies from negatives. A collage makes a great gift as a memory of a reunion or an event. Connie sent a collage of family photos with her kids to camp, and laminated them.

- *Place mats for children:* Photocopy a collage of photos and laminate it at the copy center. Use it as a place mat to remind your children of people, places, and events.
- *A "Johnny's Day" album:* Kate created an annual photo album consisting of a dozen enlarged photos of each child. The photos captured his favorite activities. She gave a copy to grandparents and godparents, and kept one for herself. Now she has "yearbooks" from the time each baby was born until his graduation from high school.
- *Photographic history book:* A life history album is a wonderful way to commemorate a birthday, an anniversary, or the death of a loved one. Copies may be distributed to friends and relatives. Personal history books can be made in two sizes—$8^1/_2 \times 11$ inches or $5^1/_2 \times 4^1/_4$ inches—and spiral bound at a copy center.

Memorabilia Simplified

Create a simple system for dealing with mementos so they do not float aimlessly around the house or office.

Keep mementos in one place: Create a yearly file for your mementos—cards, programs, postcards, and photos from friends. When you have something on your desk or bulletin board that you cannot bear to toss because it brings up a happy memory, you will have a quick place to put it. At the end of each year, place this file in a banker's box along with files from previous years.

Make an "Old Lady Box". Sharon Kristensen invented the "Old Lady Box." Each year, she collects cards, pictures, and mementos in a box. At the end of the year, she takes the box to her storage locker. When she is an "old lady," she will enjoy her memories and will have spent little time monitoring and storing them.

Save the kids' school paper and artwork. First, get a basket or container for each child's school papers. Then, once a month, encourage your child to save a few of his favorite papers and toss the rest. If the artwork is bulky, take a photo of your child beside it—reduce it to a snapshot. Buy a large acrylic box frame and put artwork in it. Hang it for a few months and then encourage your child to change it.

Look for cardboard file drawers in catalogs. Many catalogs have cardboard storage products that are useful for saving mementos. One chest has drawers labeled for 1st through 8th grades. This model works well for school mementos.

Save feel-good letters. Set up a file for nice cards, letters, and thank-you notes that make you feel appreciated. This is a great file to refer to on those days when you feel you need a boost. It'll cheer you up.

Photo Simplifiers

Taking, displaying, and storing photos is more enjoyable when you simplify the process and take away the clutter and confusion.

Make a red check mark by tips that will simplify your photos.

❑ **Create a photo supply center.**
Create a special place (shelf, drawer) for your camera equipment and supplies—cameras, carrying cases, photos, videos, film, and batteries. When a part of your material life is out of control, it is often because you do not have a "center," a place for items in one category.

❑ **Use acrylic slip-in frames.**
Sometimes the hardest part about displaying photos is getting

the photo into the frame. Inexpensive slip-in frames are a quick and easy way to view photos.

❑ **Use clear acrylic box frames.**
These frames are easy to use because they can be put on a wall in minutes. They look nicest in odd-numbered groupings.

❑ **Use a paper cutter.**
There are parts of photos you may not wish to keep. Crop off the unattractive part and enjoy what's left. Paper cutters make clean cuts and come in many sizes.

❑ **Discover the catalog *Exposures*.**
Exposures is an entire catalog of accessories for displaying, storing, and maintaining photos and mementos. (800) 572-5750.

❑ **Keep the best, toss the rest.**
Pictures capture memories. Part with photos that may negatively color your memories.

❑ **E-mail your photos.**
There are several ways to transfer photos to a computer so they can be e-mailed:

- Photos can be put on floppy disks or CD-ROM when they are developed.
- Photos can be developed and returned via the internet.
- Photos and negatives can be scanned into a computer.
- Photos can be downloaded directly from a digital camera.
- The new Advanced Processing System camera creates a special type of negative that can be easily scanned into a computer.

❑ **For Serious Simplifiers only!**
Create one fabulous photo album from your most prized photos of the past. You might choose great snapshots from several big events—vacations, birthdays, weddings, christenings. Forget the detailed system we described above. Don't do anything that takes

more than a couple of hours. Store the best of the rest of your photos in a banker's box and give some to family members. Do this project, put it aside, and get back to the joy of living in the present.

Simplifying your life can be done in little steps, one hour at a time.

DAY 26

Pare Down Your Garage

Task: *Your garage is not a junk bin. It's an important base of operations, like your kitchen and home office. Today, sort your garage items into categories—tools, paint, gardening, recreational, barbecue, and so on. As you sort, ask yourself:*

1. *Do I use it—or think I should? If not, toss it.*
2. *When I want to do a project, is this item ready to use? Am I willing to keep it cleaned and repaired? If not, toss it.*
3. *Do I have enough space for this and is it well located? If not, toss it or move it.*

After you have sorted and tossed, make a list of organizers that will streamline your garage.

Sally Field is fanatical about her garage. "Yesterday, I had three scripts to read, but I was outside cleaning the garage, making sure all of the bikes were on the right hooks. It's pathetic, but I can't work if my garage isn't straightened." Sally would feel comfortable in Connie's garage.

Everything in Connie's garage is behind white doors. Because she enters and exits the house from her garage, she wants it to be a pleasant experience. "I see this space at least twice a day and I don't want the clutter of the garage to clutter my mind." Along the back wall is a long counter with cabinets above and drawers and cabinets below. Along the side walls are tall vertical cabinets.

What is in those cabinets? One cabinet is for sports equipment, one is for camping equipment, and one is for gardening supplies. One smaller cabinet is for paint cans and another is for car washing supplies. One drawer is for basic tools, like hammers, screwdrivers, and wrenches. Another is for electrical supplies, like extension cords, and yet another is for tapes and adhesives.

Organize Your Garage

Your garage can be as clean, orderly, and functional as a room in your house. To make it work for you, ruthlessly toss the extraneous. You know what we mean—dried-up paint, carpet remnants, torn screens, piles of newspapers, outdated ski boots, and that old lawn mower.

Many rentable items are stored in garages. Always ask yourself before you buy: "Can I rent or borrow this piece of equipment?" Machines stored in garages tend to be bulky, greasy, and in need of an overhaul. Leave room for your car and frequently used tools.

Stop hunting, moving, and shoving stuff around to find what you need. After you have cleaned out your garage, buy or build the best organizers you can afford. Visit your local hardware stores, builders' supply centers, and office supply stores. Check out pressboard cabinets and talk to cabinetmakers. If you want something less permanent than built-in storage, hang wooden shelves on metal brackets on the walls. Place rows of same-sized cardboard or plastic boxes on the shelves. Label them clearly. Computer labels add uniformity.

Should I Have a Garage Sale?

It's dangerous to utter the words, "I'm going to have a garage sale." That proclamation can cause you to continue storing items in your garage forever. What are your options?

Schedule a garage sale today. An impending garage sale can motivate you to get rid of clutter. Plan one today. Set a date, collect and label items, and advertise the sale. If you have a sale and enjoy it, set a date for another one a year later.

Get real about garage sales. As you discover items for a garage sale, price them immediately and put them in a corner of your garage. Then ask yourself, "Do I want to store or trip over this junk for a whole year when I will only get a dollar (or less) for it?" A cappuccino and muffin at your local cafe costs more than you will get for that piece of junk. Maybe, it would be easier to take bags of items to a charity and get a tax deduction. Pricing garage sale items helps you get real about your stuff.

Tape a "Free" sign on it. If you have a large item—like a sofa, mattress, refrigerator, or rebuilt engine—and you don't want to have a garage sale or put an ad in the classifieds, set it on the sidewalk with a big "Free" sign. It will be gone in less than 24 hours.

Hold a garage sale with your kids. Help your kids simplify by having them select items they are willing to sell. Negotiate a price for each item and then you purchase them. Give them more for large items, like a Barbie car, and less for small items, like a plastic necklace. Then instead of having a sale, donate the recently purchased toys to charity. The children get the immediate satisfaction of having a garage sale and you get the toys recycled.

Connie's daughter, a teenager, is now on a clothing allowance. Rather than go through the hassle of selling at a consignment shop good dresses that she has outgrown, Connie buys the dresses from her daughter and donates them to the local cancer thrift shop—and then takes a write-off.

Get Smart About Cars

We spend a lot of time in cars. They have come to feel like a second home. Keep your car clean, clutter free, user-friendly, and ready to roll.

- *Carry an organized folder with local maps.* Getting lost is no fun.

- *Make a folder for registration and insurance cards.* Put the folder in the glove compartment. As you receive updated documents, discard the old ones. Make copies of the new ones for the car files in your office.
- *Create a phone book for the car.* Make a list of frequently called numbers for making calls on the road. Include directions to clients' homes or offices.
- *Get gas the same time each week.* Don't wait until you run out. It's okay to fill a half-full tank. Assigning a specific day and time of the week to do repetitive tasks relieves you from having to think about them at other times during the week.
- *Set up a cleaning schedule.* Running by the car wash on Saturdays, on your way to tennis or the farmer's market, could be a great routine.
- *Establish a maintenance schedule.* Keep a maintenance schedule in the glove compartment, in your date book (on Post-its), on your computer, or in the car manual. Many cars require tune-ups quarterly or every 4,000 miles.
- *Create three files for each car:*
  –Ownership document files: File the sales papers (pink slips), loan papers, title, and any other permanent information.
  –Car maintenance files: File the receipts from the repair shop. Know when repairs have been done so you do not do them again unnecessarily.
  –Insurance coverage files: Keep this file updated. Check with your insurance agent periodically to make sure that your coverage is adequate.

Garage and Storage Simplifiers

Your garage costs the same per square foot as your house. It is probably the largest room. So, use it wisely.

Make a red check mark by tips that will simplify your garage.

❏ **Create an Ambivalence Center in the garage.**
On Day 3, we described an Ambivalence Center, an out-of-the-

way place for things you rarely or never use and don't have the guts to give up. The Ambivalence Center—which could be a stack of lidded boxes in a corner of the garage or a special storage locker—allows you to practice living without your questionable possessions.

❑ Edit your storage locker.

By putting possessions in storage, your home and garage will be less cluttered. But a rented locker makes it possible to keep things you might normally toss out. *A Good Policy:* Every time you go to the locker, scan its contents and toss a few items. Place unwanted items outside the locker with a sign saying "Free Stuff" or "Take Me." Your castoffs will be gone in less than twenty-four hours. Build in a loft and shelves for maximum storage.

❑ Use the same white paint wherever you use white paint.

It's efficient to use the same shade of white paint for the inside of your house, the trim, the garage, and the porch. Choose a white that will blend with the other colors you choose. By going with just one shade of white, you will only need to store one can of flat and one can of glossy for touch-ups. For colored rooms, keep a small amount of paint in a can or jar, well marked with the formula and the name of the room. Simplify your paint life.

❑ Paint the inside of the garage a light color.

Garages need not be dreary. Make yours bright and cheery. Cris's husband painted the inside of their garage/workshop stark white. Transform your garage into a brighter place with a couple of buckets of paint.

❑ For Serious Simplifiers only!

One month from now, go through your garage again. Toss more *ambivalent items.* Then buy organizers for tools, gardening supplies, and sports equipment. Install them immediately!

∽

Your garage doesn't have to look like a dump site.

DAY 27

Make Landscaping Easier

Task: *A successful landscape is one that you thoroughly enjoy and is easy to maintain. Use plants that require little maintenance. Ask the nursery for three of the most successful plants in your region. Make these plants the mainstay of your garden.*

A low-maintenance landscape consists of trees, bushes, and ground covers. To add color, add a few flowering trees to highlight the seasons. Plant flowering bushes for additional low-maintenance color.

Choose flowers that don't need much deadheading or pruning. For example, impatiens are easy, durable, and will spread over a large area. Although they are annuals, they last a long time in most climates. Perennials are easier to have in the garden because they don't require replanting every year.

If you love flowers and have little time to manage them, plant them in an area that is highly visible. To get the maximum impact, plant a large area with one or two of your favorite flowers. For a tranquil look, choose just one or two colors. White flowers against a green backdrop with a touch of blue can be exquisite.

Low-Maintenance Gardening

Sunset magazine is a valuable source for ideas on creating easy-to-maintain gardens. A few tried and true basic concepts for low-maintenance gardening follow:

- *Use the toughest plants in your region.* They are the plants you often see in city median strips, county parks, and older neighborhoods. These plants are common because they never fail.
- *Give plants space.* Allow each plant to develop to its full size at the start to avoid constant pruning back.
- *Keep it simple.* The more different things you plant, the more you have to keep track of. Tasks get forgotten, plants get overlooked. Fewer is usually visually better too.
- *Mulch.* A thick layer of wood chips reduces your work load. It prevents weeds from forming and helps the soil retain moisture. Plus, it adds organic matter to the soil as it slowly decomposes. Mulch also makes the garden look neater.
- *Forget perfectionism.* Remember it is nature and nature has a life cycle.

Plant a Native Landscape

A native landscape requires little care and water. However, learning about native plants and reformatting your garden into a native landscape is time-consuming. If you are starting from scratch, consider native plants. If you have an established yard, slowly replace your old plants with native plants. If you can afford to have your whole yard replanted, relandscaping with native plants is the simplest solution.

For an introduction to native plants, start with wildflowers in your area. Opportunities for learning about native plants abound. Visit libraries and bookstores. Attend seminars. Write to the National Wildflower Research Center, 4801 La Crosse Avenue, Austin, TX 78739.

Go for Large Indoor Plants

Here's a good rule to follow: Place no more than two hefty plants in each room. Life is simpler when you live with a few large plants rather than dozens of small ones.

Connie has simplified her plant life with self-watering planters which require water only once a month. Because of the construction of the planters, she can place them on a good floor and not worry about them sweating and overflowing. To try self-watering planters, write to Planter Technology, 4007 Transport Street, Palo Alto, CA 94303-4914, for a catalogue and price list. Or call (800) 542-2282. Pots start at $9 for an 8-inch pot. Many other sizes are available.

When it comes to choosing a few special plants, select varieties that will help you breathe easier. Indoor pollution is a year-round problem, and a bigger problem in the fall and winter when windows are sealed shut. According to a NASA study on clean air, many indoor plants reduce air pollutants by filtering noxious gases.

Plants that make excellent air purifiers are aloe vera, bamboo palm, dracaena family, English ivy, peperomia, philodendrons, schefflera (umbrella plant), and spathiphyllum. Flowering plants such as Gerbera daisies and chrysanthemums also make excellent air filters.

To explore the purifying effects of plants, read Dr. B. C. Wolverton's uplifting book *How to Grow Fresh Air* (Penguin Books). This little book contains charts and photographs of the best plants for reducing specific chemical vapors.

Keep in mind, plants have a life cycle like everything else. It's okay to recycle them and start again. Our friend Kimberly simplified her life by eliminating all of her indoor plants.

Landscaping Simplifiers

If you have the good fortune to have a plot of ground, figure out ways to thoroughly enjoy it. Make maintaining a garden a form of relaxation, a meditation, not a burden.

Make a red check mark by tips that will simplify gardening.

❏ **Create a Garden Binder.**
When you purchase plants, keep information about each plant—

its name and description—in a handy binder. Include notes, such as the location of the plant in the yard, the watering schedule, the type of food the plant needs, its feeding schedule, the amount of sun and shade it needs, and recommendations from the nursery.

❏ **Keep a month-by-month garden calendar.**
For one year, record your garden activities on a calendar month by month. Examples of notations: "Fertilize the azaleas"— "Plant the impatiens"—"Prune the roses." Keep this calendar, refer to it every year, and add to it.

❏ **Add a few large outdoor pots.**
Provide color with a few large outdoor pots planted with one or two types of your favorite flowers. A few large pots are easier to maintain than several small pots or high-maintenance flower beds.

❏ **Plant an herb garden near your kitchen.**
Picking fresh herbs such as parsley, basil, rosemary, and thyme is a joy—and a convenience. Pick only the amounts you need. No more soggy parsley in the bottom of the vegetable bin!

❏ **Plant a vegetable garden.**
To simplify, plant vegetables among the flowers in your garden. There is no need to dedicate a plot just for vegetables. Succulent tomatoes and fresh garden lettuce are among the pleasures of simple living.

❏ **Create a compost pile.**
Composting can be simple. Buy a commercial compost bin and add cooking scraps and yard clippings. Keep a compost bowl in the kitchen. The compost will create a nutritious fertilizer for garden plants.

❑ **Use coffee grounds and banana peels.**
Plants love coffee grounds. Collect grounds and toss them in the garden. Banana peels around the base of roses keep the aphids away.

❑ **Reduce your lawn area.**
Replace your lawn with a low-growing ground cover such as thyme. Thyme provides a fragrant smell and needs very little water and care—you don't have to mow it! Right now, in Seattle, there is a big trend toward digging up lawns and replacing them with native ground covers.

❑ **Create a meandering stone pathway.**
One of the most inexpensive and easiest ways to dress up a patio, yard, or garden is with stepping-stones. A yard with winding paths can remind you of hiking in the woods.

❑ **Plant more shade trees.**
Trees add magic to a yard and garden. They provide good insulation. They warm your house in the winter and cool it in the summer. Plus, a few well-established trees add thousands of dollars to the value of your house.

❑ **Enjoy meals in the garden.**
Living simply means being closer to nature. When Cris and Dave visited Sweden, they enjoyed three meals a day in her cousin's flower garden. Keep several washable, no-iron tablecloths ready to throw on your outdoor table.

❑ **Spend less time tending your yard.**

- Plant drought-resistant plants.
- Set up an automatic watering system.
- Plant more perennials and fewer annuals.
- Plant more flowering shrubs and fewer flowers.
- Hire a gardener to do the heavy work, if it's cost effective.

❏ **For Serious Simplifiers only!**
Schedule an hour a week in the garden—weeding, planting, pondering. Make gardening a part of your new, simpler life.

Nobody sees a flower, really—it is so small—we
haven't the time.

—Georgia O'Keeffe

DAY 28

Get Physical!

Task: *Make an appointment on your calendar to exercise three to four times a week for an hour, or daily for 30 minutes. This is a manageable amount of time for most people. With a simple routine, you won't have to think about when to exercise—it's prescheduled!*

Exercise has enormous benefits. People who exercise live longer and lead a healthier life. In addition, they gain an hour or two of productivity each day. They have more sustained energy and are able to focus with more clarity. Our friend Kamala says, "Don't even talk to me about depression unless you are exercising at least an hour a day."

Advice from a Fitness Expert

Bruce Fountain, the owner of Fountain's Fitness, says, "First, figure out what results you want from exercise. For example, to increase your heart and lung capacity, do an aerobics workout. To improve your strength, do weight training. Exercising with machines is certainly more efficient for both weight training and aerobics. However, if going to a gym or having a gym in your home is an not option, all of the exercises below can be done anywhere. The most important part is to schedule the time."

Here is Bruce's overview of exercise for:

- *Flexibility:* Yoga is your best bet. Martial arts and aerobics classes also have a stretching component.
- *Cardiovascular endurance (heart and lung strength):* Biking, rowing, jogging, aerobics, swimming, power walking, and variable terrain hiking will get your heart rate up. Do these activities three to five times a week for 20 to 30 minutes, as recommended by the American College of Sports Medicine.
- *Muscular endurance:* Local muscle endurance is developed by low- to moderate-intensity high-repetition exercises. To target major muscle groups, do exercises using hand weights, body weight, exercise tubes, or soup cans.
- *Muscle strength:* Strength is gained by doing high-intensity exercises for short periods of time. For instance, slow-tempo push-ups develop the chest, arms, and shoulders. Wall squats develop strength in the thighs and buttocks. Yard work—lifting soil, rocks, gravel, cement, and wood— uses abdominal activity that develops strength.
- *Power:* Accelerated movement in short bursts will develop power. Power can be developed with an exercise as simple as a frog jump—exploding from a squatting position. Modified power exercises are okay for most people to do.
- *Abdominal and low-back conditioning:* Both the abdominal wall and the musculature of the lower back are responsible for the support of the lumbar spine. Pelvic tilts and reverse crunches are good beginning abdominal exercises. Straight leg lifts, full sit-ups, and front crunches are more advanced. Lying on your stomach and slowly lifting your head and chest develops strength in your lower back.

"Studies have shown that any activity is better than none at all, so if you can't get to the gym, get out and work in the yard, go for a hike in the woods, walk on the beach, or jog in the park," says Bruce.

Fitness Simplifiers

Boomers are turning fifty as we speak and Generation X-ers are not far behind. When it comes to exercise, both generations agree, "Use it or lose it!"

Make a red check mark by tips that will help you keep fit.

❑ **Hold that stretch.**
Stretching should be comfortable and relaxing—not painful. Stretch the first thing in the morning to get going, and the last thing at night, to relax before sleeping. Stretching is one of the most important exercises you can do for better health and is the most neglected part of most people's health routine. Everyone needs to stretch more whether he is a professional athlete or hasn't exercised in years. Stretching is easy to do anywhere and in any type of clothing.

❑ **Take the stairs.**
Choose stairs over elevators and escalators. StairMasters at the gym aren't the only stairs you can climb.

❑ **Park farther away.**
Save time looking for the best parking spot. The best parking spot is far away. Exercise on the way to your destination.

❑ **Create home maintenance exercises.**
Do more tasks that require physical activity—scrub floors, rake leaves, weed the garden, sweep the driveway, and wash your car.

❑ **Walk out your front door.**
Walk out your front door, walk quickly away from your house for 10 minutes, then turn around and walk back home. You will have done 20 minutes of exercise with little effort.

❑ **Exercise at your workstation.**
Sitting at a desk for long periods of time is hard on your body.

- Set an alarm. When it goes off, do standing and/or seated exercises.
- Put a Post-it note on your computer that says, "Get up and move."
- While you are on the phone, stand up and move around.
- If you have a speakerphone, use it. You will ease the strain on your neck and shoulders—and you can even stand up and stretch while you are having a conversation.

❑ **Talk while you walk.**
Catch up with friends on a nice long walk—it can be a substitute for a nice long lunch.

❑ **Find a new physical activity that brings you joy.**
Bring exercise into your life by dancing (tap, folk, swing, hip-hop), mountain climbing, Rollerblading, or swimming, to name a few ways. In the late nineties, ballroom dancing is making a comeback. What a way to have fun and exercise, too.

❑ **While exercising, control your wandering mind.**
When you are in an exercise class and your mind wanders to errands, projects, and worries, say to yourself, "Just exercise!" You will focus on your body and relieve yourself of the stress of continuous mind chatter for a few minutes.

❑ **Schedule a weekly massage.**
Support your local masseuse. A weekly massage is one of the most important things you can do for your body, mind, and spirit. Try several masseuses until you find one that is right for you. Ask for massage gift certificates for birthdays, anniversaries, and Christmas.

❑ **For Serious Simplifiers only!**
Each day, exercise for at least an hour and stretch for 15 minutes. On weekends, set aside time for recreational exercise. You

will be more relaxed and refreshed for the coming week. On your next vacation, be more physical. Plan a golf, walking, trekking, biking, river-rafting, or cross-country skiing vacation.

〜

To keep the body in good health is a duty.
Otherwise we shall not be able to keep our mind
strong and clear.

—Buddha

DAY 29

Find Out What Works

Task: *Today fill out the checklist below. It will help you see at a glance what works and what doesn't in your life. Make a copy of this list and keep it in a place where you will refer to it again (your bulletin board or date book). Add additional categories as they occur to you.*

Is this area okay? Or do I need help?

	OK	HELP!
Closet		
Love and Wear clothes exclusively	❑	❑
Closet organized	❑	❑
Accessories managed	❑	❑
Stockings	❑	❑
Belts	❑	❑
Scarves	❑	❑
Shoes	❑	❑
Jewelry	❑	❑
Clothing Systems		
Dry-cleaning System	❑	❑
Laundry System	❑	❑
Out of Season System	❑	❑
Recycling System	❑	❑
Linen Closet	❑	❑

	OK	HELP!
Kitchen		
Counters cleared	☐	☐
Storage organized	☐	☐
Love and Use items exclusively	☐	☐
Meal Planning System	☐	☐
Grocery Shopping System	☐	☐
Entertaining Menus & Setup	☐	☐
Home Office		
Mail Handling	☐	☐
Desktop Papers	☐	☐
Office Supplies	☐	☐
Bill-Paying System	☐	☐
Filing System	☐	
Current	☐	☐
Important documents	☐	☐
Estate planning	☐	☐
Tax records	☐	☐
Home improvement records	☐	☐
Insurances	☐	☐
Archives	☐	☐
Stationery and stamps	☐	☐
Ticket System	☐	☐
Gift wrapping	☐	☐
Photos	☐	☐
Subscriptions	☐	☐
Travel files and planning	☐	☐
Kids		
Kids' rooms	☐	☐
Closet	☐	☐
Desk	☐	☐
Storage	☐	☐
Kids' papers and mementos	☐	☐
Baby-sitter information current	☐	☐

	OK	HELP!
House Maintenance		
Supplies organized	❏	❏
Daily Routine	❏	❏
Weekly Routine	❏	❏
Seasonal Routine	❏	❏
Garage	❏	❏
General		
House sitter information current	❏	❏
Recycling System for Useless Stuff	❏	❏

For many years, Connie has given the Find-Out-What-Works Checklist to her clients and to the participants in her seminars. This simple list has provided people with an overview of the sticky, messy, confused areas of their lives. It has given them an opportunity to quickly say, "Yes, this area of my life is handled and I don't need to think about this much," or, "No, this area needs to be revamped and I need some ideas or time to get it under control—Help!"

At the beginning of the book, we encouraged you to put a red check mark in the boxes by the tips that you found useful. We hope you also dog-eared pages or stuck a Post-it by an important idea. All of these tools pinpoint actions you can take to get control of your life. Taken together, these steps and actions reveal your road map toward simplicity.

For Serious Simplifiers Only!

If you are highly motivated, in the next three months, tackle *all* the areas marked "Help." Some areas will take just a few minutes to simplify and organize, while others will take hours. Imagine how you will feel when the job is complete.

∽

*When you have projects to do, don't add
anything new.*

DAY 30

Get a Little Help from Your Friends

Task: *Your task for today is to call three friends and ask, "What are some ways you have simplified your life?"*

Imagine getting together with a group of friends and discussing these questions: What's driving you crazy? What fills you with the most dread? What do you miss doing most? What do you wish you could change? What works?

Recently, we sent questionnaires to friends asking them to describe ten ways they simplify their lives. Our friends generously shared their best ideas. After reading their responses, we identified five recurring themes:

- Drop perfectionism and the guilt it produces.
- Learn to say "No!" right away.
- Make a commitment to your health—eat well, exercise, and get adequate sleep.
- Edit negative people from your life.
- Avoid shopping, whenever possible.

Here are a few tips from our friends. Make a red check mark by tips that will help you simplify your life.

Connie's friends:

❏ **Elaine Dahl, law office administrator, Seattle, Washington**
"I installed a stacking washer and dryer in a closet near my teenage daughters' rooms. Now we never talk about the wash.

Also, I make forms for everything I do *repeatedly*—such as shopping for groceries and planning parties."

❏ **Vicki McLaughlin, psychotherapist, Menlo Park, California**
Vicki has four girls. "I let my kids care for themselves as much as possible. This is not abandonment—it's empowerment. My kids are clear about which responsibilities are theirs. When I offer to help with a task—like their laundry—it's a loving gift."

❏ **Eileen Bungert-Chen, small-business owner, Santa Cruz, California**
In addition to her business, Eileen has two growing boys and a husband who is deeply involved in a Silicon Valley high-tech business. "Each member of the family has a clip on the refrigerator for all of their schedules—for school, soccer, church, and special events. This tip is my best time-saver."

❏ **Susan Coan, development director, Atherton, California**
Susan has two college-age children and is involved in several volunteer activities in addition to working part-time. Each year, she takes on the leadership of one major event. "I write everything in my Day Runner in pencil. Tasks to be performed during the month are jotted down to the left of the week they must be done—then are erased when completed."

❏ **Lynn Chase, health care management consultant, Seattle, Washington**
Lynn has a blended family of college- and post-college-age young adults, an extended family that meets often, and a thriving consulting business. "When our kids are home with their friends, and relatives are coming, I post lists on my kitchen cupboards to remind myself what to do. I have menu lists, shopping lists, and activity lists (things to do with them). Life gets confusing when twenty people want my attention. Also, posting tasks encourages people to help with the chores."

❏ **Nancy Jones, image consultant, Palo Alto, California**
Nancy, a mother of four children under the age of eight, works

part-time and is an active leader in her community. To simplify, she focuses on one or two large volunteer projects a year—she doesn't juggle several small commitments. "Sunday night is desk night! That's when I make calls, do e-mail, pay bills, and fill out forms for the kids' activities. I forget about these tasks the rest of the week."

❏ **Lyn Faust, community volunteer, retired teacher, Cupertino, California**

Lyn does everything with great gusto and thoroughness. "Whenever I make reservations, place an order, cancel an activity, or return something, I jot down the date and name of the person I dealt with. Also, I keep tickets to upcoming events in a file near my calendar. When I check my calendar for the upcoming week, I get the tickets out and attach them to the front of my date book."

❏ **Jane Stocklin, president of Gamble Gardens, Palo Alto, California**

Jane is active in her children's sports and schools, and she is a community leader. Every week, Jane makes a new calendar on an $8\frac{1}{2} \times 11$–inch sheet of paper for her activities and appointments. Along the side of her calendar, she writes tasks to be completed that week. Along the bottom, she lists tasks that cannot be completed during that week, but must be pondered. She makes lists for the day from her weekly master calendar.

❏ **Nancy Walsh, substitute teacher, San Diego, California**

During most of Nancy's adult life, she was a first grade teacher and a single mom to two children. Her tip for parents: "On Sunday nights, make sandwiches—with the mayonnaise—for the whole week, and freeze them. Cut desserts into single servings and freeze them as well."

❏ **Janice Parsons, owner of The Bead Shop, Palo Alto, California**

In addition to being a single mom who is active in her community, Janice owns her own business. To simplify, Janice conscientiously cuts out *everything* she does not have to do. She buys clothes that don't need dry cleaning, she has a hairstyle that requires little maintenance, and she has manicures only on vacations.

❑ **Samantha St. Julian, psychologist, actress, artist, Independence, Missouri**

Samantha is an avid reader of current periodicals. "I use stacking trays to hold magazines. I stack ten trays on the floor and put one type of magazine in each tray. The mastheads can be seen at the front of the trays. Since the most current magazine is always on top, it's easy to find the one that needs tossing on the bottom." Her philosophy: "I always assume there's a simpler, more efficient way to do things—so I look for it."

❑ **Lois Anderson, educator, Atherton, California**

For fifteen years, in addition to being a wife and a mother of two boys, Lois has been a collector and disseminator of ideas for smoothly running a home and family. During peak family and working hours, she turns on her answering machine. "I have overcome the neurotic need to answer the phone every time it rings! I return calls in one sitting—when it is convenient for me." Another way she reduces stress is to *arrive early*. "Forget about trying to squeeze in one more errand or phone call. If you do, you will communicate that you don't care—and if you don't care, don't say yes in the first place."

❑ **Tina Mabry, computer design student, Santa Cruz, California**

Tina has raised kids, worked full-time, and is pursuing a new career. "My major strategy for simplifying is to get as much exercise as possible, eat a healthy diet, get enough sleep, look for the best in everyone, and have a regular and exciting sex life. The rest falls into place."

❑ **Jacqueline Mayer, financial planner, San Jose, California**

Jackie accomplishes more in one day than most people do in a week. For instance, most mornings, Jackie meditates and goes to the gym, then works a full day—she eats a lunch she packed the night before—and meditates again before retiring. In addition, she often has evening meetings. "Before I meditate, I sometimes put a hydrating mask on my face or a clear coat of polish on my nails to dry." To keep her mind clear she responds to requests (like our questionnaire) immediately. She doesn't waste energy thinking about incomplete tasks.

❏ **Katie Snodgrass, financial advisor, Menlo Park, California**
Katie just had her first child, has a career, and is pursuing an M.B.A. "In my Day-Timer, I keep a list of people I give birthday and Christmas gifts to. Throughout the year, I jot down ideas for gifts. I do the same for myself, so when someone asks me what I would like, I can answer on the spot."

❏ **Judy Barsky, interior designer, travel consultant, Napa, California**
Judy frequently travels for both work and pleasure. Her travel tips: "I pack with plastic bags which keep things in groups, keep items from getting dirty, and keep bottles from spilling onto other items. I always pack a laundry bag. When I buy clothes, I ask, 'Will it pack easily?' "

❏ **Toni Ahlgren, organizational consultant, St. Helena, California**
"I create lists of frequently used phone and fax numbers. I post a fax list near my fax machine and a phone list beside each phone. I also have a phone list in my car in a plastic sheet protector. In my glove compartment, I have a small binder with clients' phone numbers and directions to their houses."

❏ **Jane Willison, mother of four children under 11, Atherton, California**
Jane is a patron of the arts in every sense of the word. To run her home efficiently, in a loving and lovely manner, she has a staff and numerous organized systems. "We have a white message board in the laundry room, where the children, my husband, and the household help write their needs under headings such as Drugstore, Grocery, Office Supplies, Hardware, and Other." When Jane entertains, she prints up menus for the table. Later she puts them into a Hostess Notebook along with a record of the place setting for the dinner, the decorating motif, and comments for what to do next time.

❏ **Connie Loarie, community volunteer, Atherton, California**
Connie is a community volunteer and mother of two daughters. She increases the number of books she can read by listening to

books on tape in her car, while cooking, and while doing "mindless tasks such as bill paying."

❏ **Katherine Lerer, retired real estate broker, Palo Alto, California**
Katherine's boys are grown, so she has time for things she could not do during her child-rearing and working years. Her tips: "Start projects early and allow extra time, so you don't have to hurry at the end, which can cause you to forget something important. If you take medication, carry extras at all times. It may not be convenient to go home between activities. For travel, pack silk long underwear for cold weather—it dries quickly."

❏ **Melinda Cootsona, graphic artist, San Mateo, California**
"We put a dry-erase board on the fridge for listing leftovers. Food in the small plastic containers gets eaten and doesn't turn green."

Cris's friends:

❏ **Patricia Nichols, executive secretary, Las Cruces, New Mexico**
Patricia loves horseback riding and table tennis. "With the approval of my boss, I frequently work holidays and take weekdays off. At work, I accomplish two to four times more in eight hours without phones and interruptions—and I have the copier and printer all to myself!"

❏ **Allyson Rusu, Nordstrom designer salesperson, Sausalito, California**
Allyson lives in a cozy apartment overlooking a harbor. "To save time, I don't travel long distances for services. Instead, I go to a local grocer, dry cleaner, video store, and take-out deli. For exercise, I walk often. Walking is cheap and I don't have to drive to an exercise class."

❏ **Nancy Jean Head, painter and paper maker, Fortuna, California**
To simplify their lives, Nancy and her husband, Dick, moved

from a big city to a rural community. "I do not schedule a full calendar *ever*—it makes me anxious. Also, I do hatha yoga daily. Breathing deeply is the best relaxation and healing technique I have found."

❏ **Carol Beres, property manager, El Cajon, California**
Carol manages a commercial building in San Diego. "I make time to contribute to my church and community but have learned to say no to projects and committees that, to me, are boring and tedious. There's always a choice. No one gets fired when you're a volunteer."

❏ **Susan Marie Schustak, research director, *Dr. Dean Edell Show*, San Francisco, California**
Susan loves hiking, reading, her boyfriend, Doug, and her golden retriever, Big Jake. "I discard, sell, give away superfluous stuff regularly. I try to deal with each item (a bill, an article, a product) just once."

❏ **Kitti DeLong, gemologist-jeweler, Port Hadlock, Washington**
Kitti's passion is hunting for precious stones. "I hang my collection of ethnic jewelry on a lace-covered corkboard. I can find what I want to wear at a glance. I get great pleasure out of seeing my collection."

❏ **Diane Cowen, nurse, Santa Rosa, California**
Diane is artistic and highly organized. "For camping, I use the same menus every time. My grocery list is on the computer. Each family member has a small toiletries duffel bag with a comb, shampoo, toothbrush, thongs, and flashlight."

❏ **Kathleen Kemsley, author of *Nobody's Mother*, Alaska**
Kathleen lives in a 20 by 30–foot cabin on an acre of land. "After much searching, I made the decision not to have children. I've lost some life experiences but have gained enormous time and energy to pursue my dreams."

❏ **Barbara Hansen, professor, McLean, Virginia**
Barbara uses her Sharp Wizard for everything. "I use it for appointments, telephoning, shopping lists, my To Do list, birthdays, and much more. If I lose it, I'm dead!"

❏ **Judy Curtis, writer, lecturer, Portland, Oregon**
Judy is the author of *Living with Diabetic Complications*. She is a frequent traveler. "I pack underwear, stockings, and scarves in gallon-size Ziploc bags for easy transferring to hotel room drawers. Also, I stick to one color scheme, so I only need one pair of shoes and one handbag."

❏ **Stephanie Morrell, real estate broker, Port Townsend, Washington**
Stephanie begins her day with an hour of tai chi chuan exercises, which bring calm and focus to the remainder of her day. "To keep my life serene, I chose not to have children. Instead, I borrow them occasionally!"

❏ **Pamela Larsson-Toscher, artist, Santa Barbara, California**
Pamela is a painter and an American Sign Language interpreter. "From the time my children were young, I gave them lots of chores and made sure they did them. Now they pick up after themselves and offer to help."

❏ **Ginger Covalt, dental hygienist, Redondo Beach, California**
Ginger has one intention—self-realization. Her path is siddha yoga. "I'm a vegan, which simplifies my life a great deal. Because I only eat nuts, grains, fruits, and vegetables, meal planning is easy."

༄

I would not have anyone adopt my mode of living. I
would have each person be very careful to find out
and pursue his or her own way.

—Henry David Thoreau

Appendix

Create your own version of simple living. Throughout this book, you checkmarked tips. To make them more accessible, go back through the book and find the tips you want to remember. (If you like, you might also add tips from our friends in the previous chapter.) Write your favorite ideas down in the spaces below or on a piece of paper. Put the page number of each tip in the box, so you can refer to it quickly. Post your list and review it often.

Page

*A great task is accomplished by a series
of small acts.*

Books, Newsletters, and Websites

Develop a strategy for simplifying your life. What friends or professionals do you know who can help you? Below are some books, newsletters, and websites to explore. Benefit from other people's experiences.

Andrews, Cecile. *The Circle of Simplicity—Return to the Good Life*

Aslett, Don. *Not for Packrats Only* and *Clutter Free Finally & Forever*

Bender, Sue. *Plain and Simple—A Woman's Journey to the Amish*

Blix, Jacqueline, and David Heitmiller. *Getting a Life*

Breathnach, Sarah Ban. *Simple Abundance: A Daybook of Comfort and Joy*

Carlson, Richard and Joseph Bailey. *Slowing Down to the Speed of Life*

Cox, Connie, and Cris Evatt. *Simply Organized!*

Covey, Stephen R. *The Seven Habits of Highly Effective People*

Dacyczyn, Amy. *Tightwad Gazettes, I, II and III*

Dominguez, Joe, and Vicki Robin. *Your Money or Your Life—Transforming Your Relationship with Money and Achieving Financial Independence*

Durning, Alan. *How Much Is Enough?*

Ehrlich, Paul R. *The Population Explosion.*

Elgin, Duane. *Voluntary Simplicity—Toward a Way of Life That Is Outwardly Simple, Inwardly Rich*

Fromm, Erik. *To Have or to Be?*

Gregory, Susan. *Out of the Rat Race: A Practical Guide to Taking Control of Your Time and Money So You Can Enjoy Life More*

Lara, Adair. *Slowing Down in a Speeded Up World*

Levering, Frank, and Wanda Urbanska. *Simple Living—One Couple's Search for a Better Life* and *Moving to a Small Town: A Guidebook to Moving from Urban to Rural America.*

Liedloff, Jean. *The Continuum Concept: In Search of Happiness Lost*

Lindbergh, Anne Morrow. *Gift from the Sea*

Luhrs, Janet. *The Simple Living Guide—A Sourcebook for Less Stressful, More Joyful Living.*

Maté, Ferenc. *A Reasonable Life: Toward a Simpler, Secure, More Humane Existence*

McKenna, Elizabeth Perle. *When Work Doesn't Work Anymore: Women, Work, and Identity*

Nearing, Scott, and Helen Nearing. *Living the Good Life: How to Live Simply and Sanely in a Troubled World* and *Simple Food for the Good Life*

Miller, Ph.D., Timothy. *How to Want What You Have: Discovering the Magic and Grandeur of Ordinary Existence*

Pawson, John. *Minimum*

Popov, Linda Kavelin. *The Family Virtues Guide*

Quinn, Daniel. *Ishmael* and *My Ishmael*

Robbins, John. *Diet for a New America*

Raspberry, Salli, and Padi Selwyn. *Living Your Life Out Loud*

Rechtschaffen, Stephan, M.D. *Time Shifting: Creating More Time to Enjoy Your Life*

Saltzman, Amy. *Downshifting: Reinventing Success on a Slower Track*

Schor, Juliet. *The Overworked American: The Unexpected Decline of Leisure*

Shi, David E. *The Simple Life* and *In Search of the Simple Life: American Voices Past and Present*

Stanny, Barbara. *Prince Charming Isn't Coming—How Women Get Smart about Money.*

St. James, Elaine. *Simplify Your Life* and *Inner Simplicity*

Taylor, Robert, Susannah Seton, and David Greer. *Simple Pleasures*

Van Steenhouse, Andrea. *A Woman's Guide to a Simpler Life*

Venolia, Carol. *Healing Environments*

Willand, Lois Carlson. *The Use-It-Up Cookbook*

Yorkey, Mike. *Saving Money Any Way You Can: How to Become a Frugal Family*

Zelinski, Ernie J. *The Joy of Not Working*

Simple Living Newsletters

Simple Living—The Journal of Voluntary Simplicity. A quarterly newsletter with practical tips and real-life stories. Editor Janet Luhrs says, "Simple living is about living deliberately. You choose your experiences rather than sailing through life on automatic pilot." For a sample copy, call or write to 2319 N. 45th Street, Box 149, Seattle, WA 98103; (206) 464-4800.

A Real Life. This newsletter reminds us that we have a choice about what we let into our lives. We are all craving meaning—and the message here is you can create a meaningful life *anywhere.* Editor Barbara McNally says, "We have depended on marketers to dictate what we should value. And we are going too fast to try and keep up—faster than most of us can handle and stay healthy—cramming life in, for what? To acquire more?" Six issues a year. Send $30 dollars to 245 Eighth Avenue, Box 400, New York, NY 10011.

Messies Anonymous—Harmony in the Home through Understanding the Messie Mindset. A witty newsletter that will help you clean up your act once and for all. Editor Sandra Felton, 5025 S.W. 114th Avenue, Miami, FL 33165; (786) 271-8404.

The White Dot ($8 for 4 issues). Write to P.O. Box 577257, Chicago, IL 60657. The newsletter is about the joys of not watching television. The editor, Jean Louis, says, "Sitting in an easy chair watching Arnold Schwarzenegger is not an adventure. Knocking on your neighbor's door is."

Creative Downscaling. A newsletter on "upscale, simplified living on a downsized budget." Ten issues a year. Write to editor Edith Kilgo, P.O. Box 1184, Jonesboro, GA 30237-1884.

New Road Map Foundation is an all-volunteer, nonprofit organization that promotes a humane, sustainable future for our world. The organization was started by Vicki Robin and Joe Dominguez. For information, write to P.O. Box 15981, Dept. BK, Seattle, WA 98115; (206) 527-5114.

Building with Nature Newsletter is a 16-page bimonthly published and edited by architect Carol Venolia, author of *Healing Environments.* Carol will help you create buildings that preserve natural resources and enhance human vitality. For a sample issue, send $5 to P.O. Box 4417, Santa Rosa, CA 95402-4417.

Simplicity Websites

Simple Living Journal
www.simpleliving.com

The Simple Living Network
www.slnet.com

National Association of Professional Organizers
www.napo.net

Pierce Simplicity Study's Book List on Simple Living
www.mbay.net/~pierce/reading.htm

Center for a New American Dream
www.newdream.org

Real Goods (catalogue)
www.realgoods.com

The Work
www.thework.org

The Get Organized News
www.tgon.com

Organizing Solutions
www.wco.com/~dpmiller/index.htm

Jeff Campbell's *Household Solutions That Work*
www.thecleanteam.com

Betsey Couch's *The Kitchen Link* (recipes)
www.kitchenlink.com

Good Eats Shop-at-Home Natural Foods
www.goodeats.com

Awakening Earth
www.awakeningearth.org

YES! A Journal of Positive Futures
www.futurenet.org

The Garden
www.thegarden.net

Successful living is a journey toward simplicity and a
triumph over confusion.